CREATIVE
BIBLE LESSONS IN

FAITH ON FIRE!

CREATIVE BIBLE LESSONS IN Romans

FAITH ON FIRE!

CHAP CLARK

Youth Specialties

ZONDERVAN™

GRAND RAPIDS, MICHIGAN 49530

Creative Bible Lessons in Romans: Faith on Fire!
Copyright © 1996 by Youth Specialties

Youth Specialties Books, 300 S. Pierce St., El Cajon, CA 92020, are published by
Zondervan, 5300 Patterson Ave. S.E., Grand Rapids, MI 49530.

Library of Congress Cataloging-in-Publication Data
Clark, Chap, 1954-
    Creative Bible lessons in Romans : faith on fire! twelve ready-to-use Bible
lessons for your youth group / Chap Clark.
        p. cm.
    ISBN 0-310-20777-0 (pbk)
    1. Bible. N.T. Romans——Commentaries.   2. Bible. N.T. Romans—Study and teach-
ing.   3. Youth——Religious life.   I. Title.
    BS2665.3.C65 1996
    268'.433——dc20   95-41227

Unless otherwise indicated, all Scripture quotations are taken from the Holy Bible: New
International Version (North American Edition). Copyright © 1973, 1978, 1984 by
International Bible Society. Used by permission of Zondervan.

Edited by Noel Becchetti and Vicki Newby
Cover and interior design by PAZ Design Group

Printed in the United States of America

01 02 03 04 05 06 07 /VG/ 17 16 15 14 13 12 11 10 9

TABLE OF

CONTENTS

LIST OF WORKSHEETS

Bible-study worksheets in this book

Personal-application worksheets in this book

ACKNOWLEDGEMENTS

I'm grateful to my family—Dee, Chap, Rob, and Katie—for giving me many, many hours (of what could have been family time) to read, study, think, write, and type.

Youth Specialties is a family that has shored up my weaknesses and enhanced my strengths—I'm proud to be associated with you.

The Youth Specialties National Resource Seminar Team—Mike, Tic, Duffy, Laurie, Doug, Marv, Ray, Ridge, and Helen—is the most diligent, faithful, creative, and gifted group of people I've ever met. This book is as much ours as mine.

To my friend and editor, Noel Becchetti, go many thanks for his help in completing this project.

What *Creative Bible Lessons in Romans* Is All About, and How to Use It

One of the sobering cultural trends of the last decade among churched young people has been the decline in biblical knowledge. Youth pastors and directors, as well as church leaders in general, are noticing not only this increasing biblical illiteracy, but even a lack of interest in the Bible.

And here's the domino effect: with such apathy toward studying and reading the Bible, there will be little understanding of the truth of God's gift to us. And lack of understanding suppresses the incentive to dive into the Scriptures to see what's there. So as every June comes and goes, another class of students graduates with a less and less appreciation for and understanding of the Bible than the class before it.

Add to this the difficult task of the Christian educator—the Sunday school teacher, the youth minister or pastor, the catechist, the confirmation instructor, the CE director, or the DRE. It's your job to teach a group of young people who often have little interest in what you're teaching. You may know what they need; you also know that, once they've been drawn into the Bible, they'll see how relevant the Word of God actually is. But to get them going is a difficult task at best.

Creative Bible lessons to the rescue!

This book of twelve creative, clear, and simple-to-use lessons does two things. First, it gets all of your students into the text of the Scriptures. It sounds basic and obvious, but it is nonetheless crucial: in every lesson the words of the passage are read aloud to your class, though in a different, unique way in each lesson.

Second, the worksheets for each lesson steer your students into investigating most major themes in the book of Romans.

The goal? To let the Scriptures do the teaching—yet presented in a way that makes your task easier.

Why Romans?

Aside from the Gospels, St. Paul's letter to the church at Rome may be the most significant theological document of the New Testament. In his letter to the Romans, Paul takes pains to lay out a detailed, specific statement describing what later became known as Christianity. Christians—adolescent as well as adult—ought to be at least somewhat familiar with this complex letter, whatever their denomination or faith tradition. For it is in Romans that the apostle describes and defends fundamental New

Testament truths—the relationship of the then-new faith to traditional Judaism, the essential unity of God's people, justification by faith, and the role of the Mosaic Law, among others.

How to Use *Creative Bible Lessons in Romans*

It would be ridiculous to try to reduce the complexity of the letter's arguments, context, and technical nuances to a meaningful curriculum for youth group use. So this study isn't an explication or even a thorough overview of Romans, but only an introduction to twelve general issues—we call them "Big Ideas"—in this Pauline letter.

Here in *Creative Bible Lessons in Romans* are twelve self-contained lessons. Anyone willing to take some time to prepare a few days in advance of each meeting can facilitate the sessions; in fact, a different person may lead the lesson each week—which means you can pass this book among your volunteers and have them each pick up one of the sessions. (Just make sure you get it into their hands more than a few hours before the meeting, because some lessons require a small project to be completed ahead of time.) You'll find these sessions clearly spelled out, easy to facilitate, and simple to present.

Of course, these lessons are yours to modify however you see fit (or however your doctrine or your church board see fit). They're hardly set in stone. Think of them as tools for you to introduce your kids to the book of Romans in a creative and comprehensive way. In session three, for example, is a transparency master of the lyrics to Steven Curtis Chapman's "Miracle of Mercy." Don't like that song? Don't like Chapman? If you know a song you like better that gets the idea across to your kids, go for it. You know your tastes and your group's preferences better than I do. Choose the videos, the songs, the prayers that work for you youth group; consider the activities in this book as suggestions (of course, they work for teenagers *I* know).

What matters is this: that your students dive more deeply into God's Word.

Each lesson contains several components:

The epistle in just 12 sentences

The **Big Idea** is what you want your kids to walk away with, if they walk away with nothing else. Although each of the lessons touches on more than just one issue, most elements in the lesson point to the Big Idea.

The Big Ideas also provide continuity from lesson to lesson. Part of each lesson is to display or post them, whether by hanging, tacking, or taping on wall, whiteboard, bulletin board, whatever. Then you add each consecutive week's Big Idea to the growing list. In this way you can easily lead your group in reviewing the Big Ideas from all the lessons you've covered so far. As the weeks go by and the list grows longer, the very visible Big Ideas have a chance to sink.

On page 115, in fact, is a handout of all twelve Big Ideas you can photocopy and distribute to your kids whenever you want to—either as a preview of what's coming, or as a summary of where you've been together.

Quick—go borrow your pastor's vidcam

The **Materials Needed** box lists everything you'll need to pull off each lesson. Some items are standard, and you'll need them every time—Bibles, pens or pencils, copies of that lesson's worksheets and memory-verse cards. Other materials are specific to that lesson—a simple video you'll need to record, a transparency you need to make from the master provided in this book, a CD or cassette of a particular song, etc.

First-century Judaic-Hellenistic theology, made understandable

This is the **Overview**. And it's *only* an overview. When you open the letter to the Romans, you're talking theological diversity—with a vengeance. Consequently, this curriculum tries to deal with those aspects in Romans that are widely accepted. Still, go ahead and invest the lesson with your interpretation (or the interpretation of your church or denomination), without thinking you have to buy my synthesis of the book, hook, line, and sinker. Tweak, replace, add, kill, whatever—you know what kind of material works for your group. In fact, run some of these lessons (or parts of lessons) by your pastor or an elder to garner their input on key issues to your faith tradition that this curriculum happens to cover.

Sorry, but you can't prepare in the car on the way to church

Before the Meeting lists what you need to have in place before students walk into the youth room. There's the standard stuff: copies of worksheets to photocopy, maybe students to prep so they can facilitate small-group brainstorming, sometimes a video to cue up and so there's no distracting static and last-minute tracking adjustments to make during the meeting itself.

A few of these Before the Meeting tasks require you to take action several days prior to the meeting itself. That's the bad news (if planning is bad news)—the good news is that such advance work makes the actual lessons simple to lead and effective in their results.

Much of the advance preparation is preparing creative variations of each week's Scripture reading. Sometimes you videotape a student reading in front of or inside a synagogue (as in session three); another time you aim your vidcam at a well-known community figure who reads the chapter (session nine).

So much for logistics. Now about the theological aspect of preparation: don't teach a passage—especially in Romans—without first reading it carefully. Then, because you know your students, you'll be able to anticipate the issues that will grab them and that you can explore with them.

Hi, guys… sorry I'm late… now where are my notes?…

The **Opening** (composed of games, videos, songs, etc., depending on the lesson) should provide excitement, build community, and create interest in the lesson.

A couple of vital things to remember about starting these lessons (or *any* meeting, really):

■ The meeting starts when the first student shows up—*not* when your opening activity begins. So have your preparation completed beforehand, so you can greet and talk with students as they arrive,

■ Stride, don't stumble, into your opening. Starting with a bingo game? Know where the cards are so you can distribute them quickly—better yet, have them already laid out before the meeting. Starting with a video clip? Cue it up and adjust the tracking and sound *before* the first student arrives.

In short, the opening tells your students how well-prepared, organized, creative, and engaging your lesson will be.

A studied Bible gathers no dust

The ideal behind the **Scripture** component is that each student will have read and interacted with Romans by the time the series is over.

The *reading* of the passage is done differently—and, it is hoped, intriguingly—each lesson. If you don't like my suggestion, that's fine as long as, somehow, the Scripture is read in a way that captures your students' attention, involves them in following the text, and does not force any student to read who, for one reason or another, doesn't want to.

The *interacting* with the passage takes the form of Bible-study handouts. (On page 6 is a list of them, with their page numbers and the scriptural passage they each explore.) These page-long Bible-study handouts are best used in small groups with competent facilitators. Make sure you give copies of these Bible-study worksheets—and the corresponding Leader's Guide sheet (see below)—to your facilitators earlier in the week, so that the leaders are thoroughly prepared to lead their students in exploring the passage.

When I say *competent* facilitators, by the way, here's what I mean: facilitators who are at least somewhat skilled at asking open-ended questions, who are familiar with the week's lesson (especially with the lesson's scriptural passage), and who know and can articulate the position of your church or denomination on issues that Romans touches on.

The volunteer's friend

The **Leader's Guide** for each Bible-study worksheet explains what's behind the questions and suggests possible answers.

The commentary I've followed in writing the leader's guide is John Stott's *Romans: God's Good News for the World* (InterVarsity Press, 1994), a highly readable pastoral commentary, thorough enough to satisfy scholars, yet clear for lay teachers. There are frequent references to Stott's book in the Leader's Guides (along with page numbers for your ambitious small-group leaders).

Now do it

Just as each lesson starts with the Big Idea, each lesson ends with the **Application**—the wheels of the Big Idea, a way kids can respond practically to the truth explored in the study. For most lessons, a second worksheet is provided (the Bible-study handout being the first one)—an open-ended, thought-provoking activity that gets personal in a hurry. (On page 6 is a list of them, with their page numbers and the scriptural passage they are related to.)

Options galore

You'll find various options sprinkled throughout the lessons:

■ **Leader Hints**—suggestions for you (or your volunteer leaders) that can enhance or round out a session.

■ **For the Younger Set**—for older elementary kids or younger middle schoolers (this varies group to group, of course)—or for a group of students who particularly need more hands-on activities. Throw in one of these options when your kids need an extra push.

■ **Extra Credit**—options for intellectually or spiritually mature kids who want to go deeper. These options are usually projects that students tackle outside of the meeting.

I hope that *Creative Bible Lessons in Romans* will help you impart biblical truth in a way that makes a difference in your kids' lives—and in a way that your students (and you!) can have a good time in the process, too.

SESSION ONE

THE SOURCE OF SELF-CONFIDENCE
Romans 1:1-17

BIG IDEA
God is at work in our lives to make us pleasing and useful to him.

Overview

In this passage Paul provides us with glimpses of his motive, commitment, and calling. He also sets the stage for the remainder of the book of Romans since Paul's two main themes are contained in it: "The integrity of the gospel committed to him and the solidarity of Jews and Gentiles in the messianic community" (Stott, *Romans*, page 36).

The Big Idea of the lesson is that God is at work in our lives so that we're pleasing and useful to him. Paul's confidence in his conviction that he personally has something unique to offer to the Roman believers is unshakable. Yet he calls himself a slave (verse 1, Greek, *doulos*), and acknowledges that he receives encouragement from others. Paul's great assurance of God's leading and his response to God's call is a model for our students. The application, then, is for us to recognize that God is at work in our lives, that who we are is pleasing to God, and that we can be useful to him.

Before the Meeting

1. Preview the video clip from *Zelig* to determine its suitability for your group. By the VCR counter, the segment is 10:45 to 13:30 That's the scene in which Zelig is interviewed about his "problem" and he replies, "I just want to be liked." To cue the video by the VCR counter, set the counter on 00:00 when the first credit appears. Then fast-forward to 10:45. Cue up the video and adjust the sound before students arrive.
2. Get the **Key to Self-Confidence** worksheet (page 19) and its **Leader's Guide** (page 20) to your small-group leaders a week before the lesson.

MATERIALS
NEEDED

- 4 non-members of the youth group, a blindfold, and a half dozen gag prizes (see **Before the Meeting**, this page, point 3)
- Copies of **The Key to Self-Confidence** (page 19)
- TV, VCR, and the video *Zelig* (1983, PG)
- Paper, whiteboard, and markers (optional; see **For the Younger Set**, page 17)
- Copies of **If I Were Writing to the Romans** (page 21)
- This session's **Big Idea** written on a whiteboard, poster, etc.
- Bibles and pencils (or pens) for all students and adults
- Scripture memory verse cards (page 116)

Take a few minutes during your introduction to talk about Paul's conversion and his importance in church history. He's first mentioned as Saul in Acts 8:1 as giving approval to the stoning of Stephen and in Acts 8:3 as beginning to destroy the church. His story is picked up again in Acts 9, where he encounters Jesus on the road to Damascus and becomes a believer. In Acts 13, he was sent on his first journey into the world of the Gentiles (to all those who were not Jewish). This was the beginning of Paul's leadership and work among the people of the Roman Empire. (By the way, Act 13:9 describes how Saul's name was changed to Paul.)

3. Write this session's **Big Idea** on a whiteboard, bulletin board, poster, overhead transparency, or wherever it can catch students' eyes during the teaching session. Ideally, after the meeting add this Big Idea to a cumulative list somewhere in the room (perhaps on an empty wall) so your group can track what they've studied in Romans. If you don't have the wall space, use the master on page 115 to make a transparency to project during your review time at the beginning of each session; reveal only the Big Ideas you've studied to date.

4. Recruit four non-youth group members to be the heads for the **Opening** Guess the Heads game. For example, recruit a pastor, a graduate from your group, a parent, and a teacher (see below).

5. Recruit three students to read the following passages from Romans: 1:1-7; 1:8-13; and 1:14-17. Give them a few days to practice their passages.

Opening (15 minutes)

Play Guess the Head. Here's how: Ask for four student volunteers and take them out of the room to a place where someone is waiting to blindfold them.

While the student volunteers are out of the room, have the four "heads" sit at the front of the room. Bring the blindfolded students back in, one at a time, and explain that they're to guess who the four heads belong to—by only touching the heads. Let them explore each head for fifteen seconds.

The winner of the game is the person who correctly guesses the most identities. Hand out gag prizes for the best and worst guesses.

Scripture (25 minutes)

Give a brief overview of the context and purpose of Romans, saying something along these lines:

> **We're going to start studying a book of the Bible. Even though we call it a book, it's actually a letter from Paul, one of the most influential leaders of the early church.**
>
> **Paul not only addresses the concerns of those followers of Christ in and around Rome; he also provides a dynamic description of what it means to be a Christian. By doing this study we're going to get to know Paul, but, more importantly, we'll also get to know Jesus and understand what the Bible says about belonging to him.**

Make sure every person has the same Bible translation in front of them so that they can follow along. Have the three students you

have chosen beforehand stand up in front and read the Romans texts for this lesson.

When the Scripture has been read, break into small groups of six students or fewer. Be sure there is an adult leader in each group. Smaller groups are fine, providing you have enough trained leaders to be with every group, but try not to have more than six students per group. Hand out **The Key to Self Confidence** worksheet (page 19) and pens, and give your students time to complete the activity.

Activity: Video (10 minutes)

After your students have finished the worksheet, introduce the video clip from *Zelig* by making comments such as these:

> **This film is a fictional documentary on the life of Leonard *Zelig*—played by Woody Allen—the human chameleon. It's about a man who has had such a hard childhood that he doesn't have a real identity himself. He simply becomes whomever he's with: an obese man, a black musician, a major league baseball player. This clip lets us in on his problem.**

Show the clip. Then say,

> **When Leonard Zelig was asked, "Why do you change?" he said, "It's safe. I want to be liked." Later in the movie Zelig says, "Ever since I was a child, I've always wanted to fit in. I was afraid I wouldn't have a place to belong. I put all my effort into being like those around me. *After a while, I couldn't control my transforming to where I'm now.* Now I don't even know who I am."**
>
> **We all want to be liked, and we're all a bit like Zelig, in our own ways. But Paul was different—he was confident of God's power to love him and God's desire to use him in a unique way.**

Romans 1:6 says, "And you also are among those who are called to belong to Jesus Christ." Jesus Christ has called you and me to trust him with our identities because we belong to him. Just as Paul was confident in the truth of God's gospel, we can be sure of this: God has made each of us unique, and he wants us to have quiet yet solid confidence that who we are is pleasing and useful to him. You don't need to work to fit in with Jesus. He already knows all about you, and he loves you right now, just the way you are.

Application (10 minutes)

Hand out copies of **If I Were Writing to the Romans** (page 21).

Instruct the students to imagine they're preparing to write to some followers of Christ in a foreign country, just like Paul did. Have them fill out the worksheet so they'll have a summary of their credentials.

Encourage them to take their handouts home and to display their worksheets where they can periodically look at them, to be reminded of God's work in their lives.

Go over the memory verse, hand out verse cards, restate the lesson's Big Idea, and display the poster.

Close with a time of prayer by having your students get with two other people, take two minutes to discuss prayer needs, and pray either out loud or silently for one another.

Romans 1:1-17
The Key to Self-Confidence

The book of Romans is actually a letter from Paul to the Christians living in and around Rome. Like any letter (or any book in the Bible), it's important to get to know the human author and see why he's writing. This first chapter gives us a glimpse into the life and ministry of Paul.

---

1. List nine things we learn about Paul from this passage.

    a. Paul's role (verse 1)

    b. Paul's title (verse 1)

    c. Paul's position (verse 1)

    d. Paul's job or calling (verse 5)

    e. Paul's commitment (verses 9-10)

    f. Paul's desire (verse 10)

    g. Paul's talent or gift (verse 11)

    h. Paul's motivation (verses 14-15)

    i. Paul's reason for confidence (verse 16)

2. Paul believes that—
- ❏ God can use anybody for this stuff, so I don't really matter.
- ❏ God does all the work; I just get out of the way.
- ❏ I've been called and gifted by God to make a difference in the world, using my gifts to the maximum.

Why did you choose the answer you did?

3. Place an X where you think Paul fits on this scale between humility and arrogance.

Humble   Arrogant and cocky

Why do you think Paul fits there?

4. Verse 17 summarizes the whole book of Romans by helping us to know what's revealed by the gospel of God:

> For in the gospel a righteousness from God is revealed, a righteousness that is by faith from first to last, just as it is written: "The righteous will live by faith."

Rewrite this verse in your own words (*righteous*, by the way, means good, pure, holy).

The Key to Self-Confidence
L E A D E R ' S G U I D E

Introduction Have a volunteer read the introductory sentences.

1 Have the group work together on the first question. Avoid having the same students always answering.

Here are the answers:

a. servant of Jesus Christ (or slave, a better translation of the Greek word *doulos*)

b. apostle (a name Jesus personally gave to the twelve disciples in Luke 6:12-16, and one which Paul also received from Christ)

c. set apart (see Galatians 1:15 where Paul states he was set apart from birth)

d. to call people from among all the Gentiles (anyone not Jewish; in other words, the rest of the world)

e. to be a servant of God with his whole heart

f. to see the Roman believers

g. his ability to impart a gift

h. his eagerness to preach because he felt an obligation toward everyone

i. he wasn't ashamed of the gospel

2 and 3 Ask the students to do these questions individually and then share their responses with the small group. These questions especially focus on verses 11, 14, and 15.

Although Paul is very confident, he seems to know the balance between self-righteous arrogance and abject humility because of Christ: he is able to give a spiritual gift (verse 11), yet he is obligated to, among others, the foolish (verse 14).

4 Discuss the verse and the directions before you invite students to paraphrase the verse. When you believe they understand, ask them to work on their own for a brief period before sharing their answers.

Question 4 looks at what Paul calls the "gospel of God" (1:1). To paraphrase Paul, this gospel is what God spoke of in the Old Testament Scriptures through the prophets. These prophets, wittingly or unwittingly, spoke of Christ—their ultimate message was about Jesus. In his human nature Jesus was a descendant of David; also, through the Spirit of holiness—and demonstrated by his resurrection from the dead—he was declared with power to be the Son of God (1:4). God, therefore, desires to make his people righteous—that is, good, holy, and pure. Righteousness comes by faith in Christ.

Romans 1:1-17

IF I WERE WRITING TO THE

ROMANS

1. My three best qualities are . . .

   1.

   2.

   3.

2. I can be a good friend to people because . . .

3. God has made me with the ability to . . .

4. My greatest desire when it comes to following Jesus is . . .

5. The three ways I see Jesus Christ working in my life are . . .

   1.

   2.

   3.

6. If I could choose the way for Jesus to use my gifts, talents, and interests to change the world for God, it would be . . .

SESSION TWO

SO YOU THINK YOU'RE GOOD?
Romans 1:18 - 3:31

BIG IDEA
Every person is a rebel, but God has made a way to change us through faith.

Overview

This is a long passage, loaded with theological content. The Big Idea of the lesson summarizes Paul's position that all people are sinners in need of mercy, and that works (that is, doing good) will never satisfy the justifiable wrath of God.

Here are the key elements of the lesson: a definition for sin; the relationship between sin (humanity's rebellion against God) and sins (the way we act as a consequence of our rebellious nature); humanity's inability to reconcile our broken relationships with God; the futility of trying to please God on our own merit; and the righteousness that comes through faith in Jesus Christ.

Before the Meeting

1. Get the **Anatomy of a Rebel** worksheet (page 27) and its **Leader's Guide** (page 28) to your small-group leaders a week before the lesson.
2. Write this session's **Big Idea** on a whiteboard, bulletin board, poster, overhead transparency, or wherever it can catch students' eyes during the teaching session. Ideally, after the meeting add this Big Idea to a cumulative list somewhere in the room (perhaps on an empty wall) so your group can track what they've studied in Romans. If you don't have the wall space, use the master on page 115 to make a transparency to project during your review time at the beginning of each session; reveal only the Big Ideas you've studied to date.
3. Pick four good readers to practice and present three passages each:

   ■ Romans 1:18-23; 2:5-11; and 3:1-8
   ■ Romans 1:24-27; 2:12-16; and 3:9-18
   ■ Romans 1:28-32; 2:17-24; and 3:19-25
   ■ Romans 2:1-4; 2:25-29; and 3:26-31

MATERIALS NEEDED

- Whiteboard and markers
- Copies of **Debate Preparation** sheets (pages 29-32). These are four different sheets; make enough copies of each sheet for a quarter of your group
- Adults: a moderator and 1-3 judges (see **Debate**, page 24)
- 4 prizes for debaters
- 4 older students as debaters (optional; see **For the Younger Set**, page 24)
- Copies of **Anatomy of a Rebel** (page 27)
- Bumper-sticker-sized posterboard and markers
- This session's **Big Idea** written on a whiteboard, poster, etc.
- Bibles and pencils (or pens) for all students and adults
- Scripture memory verse cards (page 116)

for the YOUNGER SET

Recruit and prepare older students to be the debaters. Your students can still break up into groups to discuss strategy, but the older students can be the group representatives during the debate. Youths will remain interested as long as they have the chance to take sides and root for their positions.

▼ ▼ ▼ ▼ ▼ ▼ ▼ ▼ ▼

Let your readers know that as soon as the class is finished reviewing the previous lesson, they're to take their positions, one in each corner of the room. After the leader has instructed the class to turn to the passage of the week and students have located it, the readers should narrate their assigned passages in sequence and without pause between readers until the entire text has been read.

4. Recruit an adult moderator and four adult judges for the **Are People Good or Evil?** debate (see below). If you plan to use the option for younger students, also recruit four older teens.

5. Cut out enough bumper sticker-sized posterboards for every student that is expected.

Opening (5 minutes)

Play Who's Good, Who Isn't. Here's how it works: Have everyone stand in the middle of the room. Read from the following list of names, one at a time, asking students to move to one side of the room if they think the person is good, and to the opposite side if they think the person isn't. All players make individual choices and must vote one way or the other.

Here's the list:
- Abraham Lincoln
- The current president of the United States
- The student's school principal
- Adolf Hitler
- Mother Teresa
- Justices on the Supreme Court
- Members of the Supremes
- Martin Luther King
- Ghandi

(*Add your own: e.g., local sports or political figures; current television, rock, or movie stars*)

After the game, ask the following questions:
- **Who do you think is the best person? Why?**
- **Who do you think is the worst person? Why?**
- **How do you know what these people are really like?**
- **Are some people basically good and others basically bad? Why?**

Activity: Debate (30 minutes)

Divide the class into as many as four groups (less with a small class) who will debate "Are People Good or Evil?" Each group will have five minutes to review its **Debate Preparation Handouts** (pages 29-32) and to choose a representative from the group to support the position they've been given during the debate.

Students can add their own ideas; groups aren't restricted to the suggestions or strategies on the handouts.

When the groups are ready, seat the judges, hand over the floor to the moderator, and start the debate. Each debater will have 90 seconds to present his or her most compelling case. After all four have made presentations, give each an additional 90 seconds to rebut the others. Keep the debate moving and lively.

Following this portion, your moderator can give the students who are observing opportunities to ask questions of any debater. Instruct the moderator beforehand to evenly distribute questions among the four participants.

Following the questioning, have the judges award simple prizes to all four debaters—in categories such as most logical, best prepared, most compelling, and quickest on his or her feet.

Have a few willing students share which arguments made the most sense to them and why. List the best arguments for each position on a whiteboard.

Scripture (20 minutes)

First, review the **Big Idea** from the last session. Do this every week to provide continuity between the lessons. Don't display the posters of the Big Ideas until they're mentioned by the students. As the weeks go by, the Big Ideas will become more familiar.

The assigned Scripture readers should be in place in the four corners of the room, ready to read. Ask the students to open their Bibles to Romans 1:18 and to follow along with the readers.

Return students to their debate teams; assign an adult leader to each team. Have the groups complete the **Anatomy of a Rebel** worksheet (page 27).

Application (5 minutes)

After the students have completed the worksheets, have each group share its conclusions with the whole class, focusing especially on the bumper stickers they created.

Introduce the memory verse, hand out verse cards, restate the lesson's Big Idea, and display the poster.

Close with a prayer time which centers on the content of the bumper stickers. Encourage students to display their bumper stickers in their rooms as a reminder of the lesson.

ANATOMY OF A REBEL

The first step in getting healthy is to recognize our need for healing. In Mark 2:17 Jesus said, "It is not the healthy who need a doctor, but the sick. I have not come to call the righteous, but sinners." The first step in Alcoholics Anonymous is "to admit that one is powerless over alcohol—one's life has become unmanageable." This lesson looks at how God sees us and what he's done about it.

The last lesson left us with a summary of Paul's letter to Romans: "In the gospel a righteousness from God is revealed" (1:17). That is, the gospel shows us how much God wants to make us his friends, and how he's come to see us as righteous—that is, as clean, pure, and good.

But why is this necessary? Hasn't God always seen me as good?

---

1. What's the wrath of God?

2. Romans 1:20 says that we are without excuse. What are two things that this verse indicates are plain to everyone, whether we admit it or not?

1.

2.

3. Those who decide against taking God seriously are called rebels, because they are in rebellion against God. What are the consequences (results) of rebellion that Paul identifies in the following verses of chapter 1:

■ Verse 21

■ Verse 23

■ Verse 24

■ Verse 25

■ Verses 26-7

■ Verse 28

■ Verses 29-32

What do you think is the root cause of this progression of consequences?

4. To the Jews, circumcision was the sign of the relationship between God and the people of Israel. Paul says that the Jews thought they were morally superior to other people because of circumcision (see 2:17-21). Consider these questions Paul asks:

■ *"You who preach against stealing, do you steal?" (2:21)*
■ *"You who say that people should not commit adultery, do you commit adultery?" (2:22)*

What is Jesus' perspective of this as he taught it in Mathew 5:27-28?

5. What is Paul's main point in Romans 2? (check the single best answer)

❑ Some people are better than others.
❑ Religious people are closer to God and more holy than nonreligious people.
❑ We're all in the same boat as sinners who rebel against God.
❑ Some do good, others do bad, and that's life.

Now compare your answer to Romans 3:9-10.

6. Using the posterboard and markers provided, write a bumper sticker that expresses Romans 3:22-23 in your own words.

ANATOMY OF A REBEL — LEADER'S GUIDE

Have a volunteer read the introductory paragraph that begins the lesson. Then ask students to complete Question 1 by themselves, then discuss their answers as a group. Repeat the process for each question.

1 God's wrath is different from human anger, which is often impulsive, vengeful, and explosive. God's wrath—a holy hostility to evil—focuses on the godlessness and wickedness of people who suppress the truth. When humanity denies that God exists, our rebellion is the ultimate form of wickedness and evil.

2 Since creation, God's power (the kind of power that only God can have) and divine nature (what God is like as expressed in creation—beauty, order, majesty) have been obvious to all. See Psalm 19:1 and Isaiah 6:3 as further support of this idea.

3 Paul outlines a progression of rebellion's consequences. Here are the answers to this section:

- ■ 21 . . . . Our hearts are darkened, we become fools
- ■ 23 . . . . We worship idols
- ■ 24 . . . . Sexuality and sensuality become an obsession
- ■ 25 . . . . Created things replace the Creator as objects of worship and adoration
- ■ 26-27 . . . . Homosexuality and other sexual sins multiply
- ■ 28 . . . . God hands us over to our rebellion
- ■ 29-32 . . . . Envy, murder, strife, deceit, malice, etc.

The root cause of this progression is our unwillingness to look toward God as our God.

4 Romans 1:14 makes it clear that Paul is talking to every human being who ever lived. Encourage your students to look for points in Paul's argument that specify we're all in the same boat.

5 This question helps students recognize that no one is any better than anyone else when it comes to being holy, pure, or righteous.

6 and 7 We're all in the same boat.

8 Hand out paper for your students to develop rough drafts of their bumper stickers. When they have ideas developed, hand out the posterboard and have them make bumper stickers for their walls at home.

DEBATE PREP I
Romans 1:18-3:31

ALL PEOPLE ARE
EVIL

1. The expression "I'm only human" implies that people can't help but do wrong.

2. When given the chance to steal, every person will steal, if they don't think they'll get caught.

3. If a waiter makes a mistake on a dinner bill that saves a customer $20, every customer will keep silent.

4. Little children don't need to be taught how to hit, cry, or say "No!"

Other ideas:

Romans 1:18-3:31

Some People Are *Good,* Some Are **EVIL**

1. As young as preschool age, some kids are naturally nice and others are bullies.

2. From the time we're young, we learn that there are some people who are very friendly and there are others who are mean and harsh.

3. For every really bad person, there's a really good one. For example, for every Hitler, there's a Mother Teresa.

4. Whether due to upbringing or genetics, some people are just plain evil. This is why we have police—to protect good people from evil people.

Other ideas:

DEBATE PREP 3
Romans 1:18-3:31

Everybody Is Basically

1. When babies are born, they're born in the image of God. They're pure and good. It's the evil influences of the outside world that make people do bad things.

2. If someone gets hurt or needs help in public, there are always more than enough people to help him or her out.

3. It's a fact that more people are volunteering to help others than ever before.

4. If you look hard enough at someone, you can see his or her inner goodness. Everybody has a good heart inside.

Other ideas:

DEBATE PREP 4

Romans 1:18-3:31

People Choose to Be *Good* **or to Be** **BAD**

1. Every time we come across a problem where we have to decide what to do, we have a choice. Sometimes we do what's right, and sometimes we do what's wrong. But we make the choice.

2. Little kids begin making choices between right and wrong early in their lives. The patterns they develop when they're young influence how good they will be when they grow up.

3. A newspaper article said that we all have the capacity for both good and evil, and we decide, depending on the circumstances.

4. Everybody is basically the same—we all sometimes choose to do good and sometimes choose to do wrong. But that's human nature.

Other ideas:

SESSION THREE

TRUST, THE KEY TO FAITH
Romans 4:1-25

BIG IDEA
Faith is having confidence that God is still working on me.

Overview

Paul changes direction in his argument for justification by faith in the fourth chapter of Romans. He's anticipating the objections of Jews who have been taught all their lives that Abraham was justified by his obedience to the law. The message Paul brings hasn't changed, but the application of history is new.

The basic thrust of Paul's argument is that Abraham was declared righteous by God *before* he underwent the rite of circumcision (verses 9-10), which is the mark of faithfulness to the Jews. This is where Paul begins the process of weaving the Jewish and Gentile believers into one family.

Paul argues that, because Abraham believed God by faith before his circumcision, he is the father of both the uncircumcised (i.e., the Gentiles who have faith in God) and the circumcised (the Jews). To the Jewish mind this was heresy; they counted Abraham as *only their* father, which set them apart from the rest of the world.

Paul's final words echo what he's been saying throughout this passage—the promise to Abraham is universal in scope but is awarded only to those who have the faith of Abraham. God will credit righteousness to those of us who have faith in God's promise, which was ultimately fulfilled when he raised Jesus our Lord from the dead (verse 24).

Before the Meeting

1. Preview the video clip from *Rocky III* to determine its suitability for your group. By the VCR counter, the segment is 38:70 to 40:15. That's the scene in which Rocky Balboa and his wife, Adrienne, are on a beach after he has apparently given up. To cue the video by the VCR counter,

MATERIALS
NEEDED

- TV, VCR, and the video *Rocky III* (1982, PG)
- Video of an adult reading Romans 4 inside or in front of a synagogue (see **Before the Meeting**, this page, point 2)
- Markers
- Copies of **God's Working on Me!** (page 37)
- Enlarged version of the map found on **God's Working on Me!** (page 37)
- Cutout figures of Jesus—one for each student—and Scotch tape (optional; see **For the Younger Set**, page 35)
- A CD or tape of the song "Miracle of Mercy" on Stephen Curtis Chapman's album *Heaven in the Real World* (Sparrow, 1994)—and a CD player or tape deck
- Overhead transparency of the lyrics to **Miracle of Mercy** (page 40)—and an overhead projector
- Copies of **My Journey with Jesus** (page 39)
- Overhead transparency of the **Prayer of Confession** (page 41)
- This session's **Big Idea** written on a whiteboard, poster, etc.
- Bibles and pencils (or pens) for all students and adults
- Scripture memory verse cards (page 116)

set the counter on 00:00 when the first credit appears. Then fast-forward to 38:70. Cue up the video and adjust the sound before students arrive.

2. Videotape an adult (someone the students will recognize and like) reading Romans 4 inside of or in front of a synagogue. Remember to get permission from the synagogue before you proceed.

3. Get the **God's Working on Me!** worksheet (page 37) and its **Leader's Guide** (page 38) to your small-group leaders a week before the lesson.

4. Write this session's **Big Idea** on a whiteboard, bulletin board, poster, overhead transparency, or wherever it can catch students' eyes during the teaching session. Ideally, after the meeting add this Big Idea to a cumulative list somewhere in the room (perhaps on an empty wall) so your group can track what they've studied in Romans. If you don't have the wall space, use the master on page 115 to make a transparency to project during your review time at the beginning of each session; reveal only the Big Ideas you've studied to date.

5. Make an enlarged replica of the map found on the **God's Working on Me!** worksheet (page 37).

6. Cue the tape or CD to "Miracle of Mercy" and test for volume, clarity, etc. Use the master on page 40 to make a transparency of the lyrics. Check the overhead projector to be sure it works. (Have a spare bulb handy.)

7. If you're going to do **For the Younger Set** option, prepare one cutout figure of Jesus for each student.

I HAVE FOUGHT THE GOOD FIGHT... I HAVE KEPT THE FAITH.
2 TIMOTHY 4:7

Opening (10 minutes)

Show the clip from *Rocky III*. Set up the scene by explaining the following:

Rocky Balboa has lost his title as heavyweight champ to Clubber Lang, and he's hired his former opponent, Apollo Creed, to train him for a rematch.

Rocky goes to Southern California to train, but during the training he realizes that he has lost the eye of the tiger—the hunger to compete. We're going to watch a scene showing Rocky's wife Adrienne and Rocky on the beach after he's given up.

After you've shown the clip, ask the kids to get together with two others and discuss these two questions:

■ **Why did Rocky want to quit?**
■ **What's the most important thing Adrienne said to Rocky that made him change his mind?**

After a few minutes, pull the groups back together to report what they shared. End by stating,

Rocky was afraid that he wasn't the same fighter that won the title, and he was afraid of Clubber Lang. Adrienne wanted to encourage him by letting him know that he wasn't alone—there were others who were there for him and believed in him. But he still had to believe in himself.

Scripture (30 minutes)

Review the Big Ideas from Sessions 1 and 2. Give students the opportunity to remember them before displaying the posters.

Play the video of Romans 4 being read in side or in front of a synagogue. Have your students follow along in their Bibles.

Hand out the **God's Working on Me!** worksheets (page 37) and pens. Break your kids into small groups with at least one adult leader for each group and complete the worksheets. When the groups begin to discuss question 5—how close they feel to Jesus—post the enlarged version of the map in the front of the room. After each small group does its work, a representative from each group will transfer his or her small group's information to the jumbo map up front (see page 38, **Leader's Guide**, questions 4-5). Give each representative a marker of a different color. Of course, no positions on the map should be identified by students' names.

Application (20 minutes)

Segue into the application by saying,

The Big Idea for this lesson is, "Faith is having confidence that God is still working on me." Sometimes—maybe most of the time—it feels like everything is on our own shoulders. But having faith means trusting God to keep working in us, and loving Christ enough to obey. It's not how close we feel to him that matters; it's how close he stays to us, even when we don't feel it.

Play the song "Miracle of Mercy," which emphasizes the fact that Christian faith is a matter of trusting God, not doing the activities of a Christian. Introduce the song by saying,

This song talks about the grace of God. Grace is God's incredible love for us even when we don't deserve it because, on our own, we can't earn God's respect or love. Even though we fail a lot, God still loves us. That's what grace is all about.

for the YOUNGER SET

This activity takes a little more time to prepare than usual, but your students will be left with a long-lasting image — so it'll be worth it. Hand a small cutout of Jesus (this can be a simple stick figure with Jesus' name written across the front) to each student. Also give everyone a piece of Scotch tape to loop inside out and attach to the back.

Invite the kids to come up front to the enlarged map and stick their Jesus cutouts right next to one of the figures added during the previous exercise. After everyone has finished, ask them to look at the place where they marked the map. They will see that Jesus is standing right beside them.

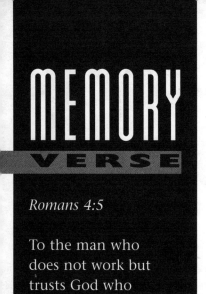

Romans 4:5

To the man who does not work but trusts God who justifies the wicked, his faith is credited as righteousness.

Place the lyrics transparency (page 40) on your overhead projector. Darken the room as much as possible. Have the kids listen to the song and prayerfully consider the meaning of the words.

Let the song be followed by a period of silence. Then, turn on the lights and read Romans 4:20-21 to them.

Hand out copies of **My Journey with Jesus** (page 39). Have students draw stick figures at approximately the same places they did previously. On the same map, ask each student to draw another figure which represents where he or she wants to be in his or her relationship to Jesus. Have them complete the question on the bottom of the handout.

Invite them to take their maps home and display them where they can regularly see them.

Introduce the memory verse, hand out verse cards, restate the lesson's Big Idea, and refer to the poster.

Use an overhead transparency to recite together **Prayer of Confession** (page 41).

Romans 4:1-25

GOD'S WORKING ON ME!

1. In verses 4-5, Paul talks about the difference between a gift and an obligation. What's the difference?

   The point Paul is making in these verses is—

2. Verse 18 says, "Against all hope, Abraham in hope believed." Why was his faith against all hope?

3. We live after the resurrection (verses 23-25), but Abraham lived long before Jesus was born. Read verses 23-25. What advantage do we have over Abraham?

4. What area is the hardest for you to trust God with? (Use abbreviations or "code" if you want to keep your response confidential, just between you and God.)

   Why?

5. On the map below, draw a stick figure that represents how close to or how far away from Jesus you are right now.

Romans 4:1-25
GOD'S WORKING ON ME!
LEADER'S GUIDE

In this chapter, Paul chooses two heroes of Israel, Abraham the father of faith and David the great king, to exemplify his point of justification by faith. It's interesting that Matthew also begins his Gospel with these same two individuals. There are two reasons for this:

- The gospel Paul preaches is not new; it has been the faith of Israel and now continues in Christ.
- He wants to connect the gospel to its Jewish roots and history.

The chapter presupposes a knowledge of Abraham's life. Before you begin the worksheet, cover four key episodes with your kids:

1. God called Abraham to leave the land of Ur to go to a new land although Abraham didn't know where it was (Genesis 12:1-4).
2. Although he didn't have any children, God promised to bless Abraham with so many children they would be a nation (Genesis 13:14-18). By trusting God to fulfill his promise, Abraham was justified before God.
3. Abraham was ninety-nine and his wife Sarah was ninety when their son was finally born. Isaac's circumcision was a sign of the covenant relationship between God and Abraham's descendants (Genesis 17:1-11).
4. God tested Abraham by asking him to sacrifice his son. Abraham's obedience reconfirmed his trust in God's promise (Genesis 22:1-19).

1 The difference between an obligation and a gift is that the first is earned while the second is given only because of the generosity of the giver, not because the person receiving it earned it or deserved it in any way. Paul makes it clear that righteousness is a gift from God.

2 "Against all hope, Abraham in hope believed" (verse 18). Abraham believed God in spite of the fact that he and Sarah were too old to have children.

3 We have an advantage over Abraham because we have seen the fulfillment of God's promise, especially the resurrection of Jesus. Abraham believed but the fulfillment of God's promise was still in the future.

4 and 5 Be careful with these highly personal questions. Don't pressure kids to share their answers. When the individual maps have been shared by those who wish to do so, have the small group prepare a composite map that indicates the positions of everyone in the group—without noting individual names. This will be used later in the lesson (see **Scripture**, page 35).

Romans 4:1-25

MY JOURNEY WITH JESUS

1. On the map, draw a stick figure which depicts how close you are to Jesus.

2. Draw a stick figure which depicts how close you *want* to be in relationship to Jesus.

The Big Idea of Romans 4 is, "Faith is having confidence that God is still working on me." God is the one that makes us grow; our job is to work at learning to trust him. The more we grow in trusting Jesus, the closer we will get to him.

3. What specifically are you going to do that will help you grow in your trust of Jesus?

Miracle of Mercy

If the truth was known and a light was shown
    On every hidden part of my soul
Most would turn away, shake their heads and say
    "He still has such a long way to go"
If the truth was known you'd see that the only good in me
    Is Jesus, oh, it's Jesus
If the walls could speak of the times I've been weak
    When everybody thought I was strong
Could I show my face if it weren't for the grace
    Of the one who's known the truth all along
If the walls could speak they'd say that my only hope was the grace
    Of Jesus, the grace of Jesus
But, oh the goodness and the grace in Him
He takes it all and makes it mine
      and causes his light in me to shine
And he loves me with a love that never ends
    Just as I am, not as I do
Could this be real, could this be true
    This could only be a miracle
This could only be the miracle of mercy

PRAYER OF CONFESSION

Leader: God, we have tried to live life on our own.

All: Forgive us, Lord.

We have left you behind as we go through our days.

Forgive us, Lord.

We have lived as if you're not real.

Forgive us, Lord.

We have lived as if you do not exist.

Forgive us, Lord.

Open our eyes so we can see you as we go about our daily activities.

Help us, our Lord.

We need to experience your love, forgiveness, and power.

Help us, our Lord.

God, give us the soft hearts of people who are forgiven.

Touch us, Lord, so we can glorify you now and forever.

God, we have tried to live life on our own.

Forgive us, Lord. Amen.

SESSION FOUR

THE GIFT OF FAITH
Romans 5:1-21

BIG IDEA
Real faith brings peace with God.

Overview

Now that Paul has laid the ground work for bringing the Jewish and Gentile believers together (a theme that winds throughout the rest of the book), he brings up the benefits of faith.

The first half of the chapter (verses 1-11) identifies three benefits of justification through faith in Christ: we have peace with God, we receive God's grace, and we have joy.

The second half (verses 12-21) contrasts the gift of justification through Christ against the condemnation that came through Adam.

Scholars disagree about the content of verses 12-21, but there's no doubt that Paul is at least indicating that we all are condemned unless we receive the gift of God's grace that is available through faith in Jesus Christ.

Before the Meeting

1. At least two weeks before this lesson, recruit two students to perform **The Gift** (page 50). Get the scripts to them well ahead of time and have them rehearse with you at least twice before their performance. The skit's not long, but to be effective, your actors must know their lines well.

2. Inform kids in advance that they should bring wrapped gag gifts for a gift exchange. Bring enough extra gifts—including a few nice ones—so that every student will get one.

3. Prepare small numbered slips of paper. Only use as many numbers as you have kids participating.

4. Get the **Greatest Gift** worksheet (page 47) and its **Leader's Guide** (page 48) to your small-group leaders several days before the lesson.

MATERIALS
NEEDED

- A few wrapped gifts (see **Before the Meeting**, point 2)
- Numbered slips of paper in a "hat" for the gift exchange (see **Opening**, page 44)
- Two copies of the sketch **The Gift** (page 50) and a prop: a really nicely wrapped gift
- Copies of **The Greatest Gift** (page 47)
- An adult volunteer to be the Iceman or Icewoman (optional; see **For the Younger Set**, page 45)
- Copies of **A Thank-You Note to God** (page 49)
- This session's **Big Idea** written on a white-board, poster, etc.
- Bibles and pencils (or pens) for all students and adults
- Scripture memory verse cards (page 116)

5. Write this session's **Big Idea** on a whiteboard, bulletin board, poster, overhead transparency, or wherever it can catch students' eyes during the teaching session. Ideally, after the meeting add this Big Idea to a cumulative list somewhere in the room (perhaps on an empty wall) so your group can track what they've studied in Romans. If you don't have the wall space, use the master on page 115 to make a transparency to project during your review time at the beginning of each session; reveal only the Big Ideas you've studied to date.

6. Recruit an adult who is a stranger to your kids to play the part of an Iceman (see **For the Younger Set**, page 45).

7. Have your student actors set their stage so they're ready to begin right after the opening game.

Opening (15 minutes)

Have a gift exchange. Here's how it works: Pile all of the gifts in the center of the room for the gift exchange and have students draw numbers out of a hat. Number one picks whichever gift looks most appealing, opens it, and shows it to everyone. The next person has the option of taking a bird in the hand—the first player's unwrapped gift—or of going hunting—picking an unwrapped gift from the pile. If the first player is left empty handed, he or she chooses another unwrapped present. In the following round, play continues in the same way until someone chooses an unwrapped present. Choosing an unwrapped present marks the end of a round. The exchange continues until all of the gifts have been opened.

You can add a twist by adding a three-minute blitz at the end when kids can trade with anyone else. When the three minutes are up, everyone keeps the gift he or she has.

Activity: Sketch (15 minutes)

At this point have the student volunteers perform **The Gift** (page 50).

Following the sketch, set the actors (who will still be in their roles as Bob and Sue) in front of the group. Tell your kids to imagine that it's the day after the concert. Bob got a seat in the back that allowed him to see Sue sitting in the front row with Kevin.

Later he talked to her and found out about the gift.

The kids can ask Bob and Sue questions or give them advice. If the discussion drags, throw in a few questions like these:

■ **Bob, how did you feel when Sue told you she wanted to give you the gift?**
■ **Were you mad at him, Sue?**
■ **What have each of you learned from this?**

Wrap up with a statement or two emphasizing the value of gifts, especially from those we care about and trust.

Scripture (20 minutes)

Review the last three Big Ideas and display them up front as you have in past lessons.

Use Tag Team Scripture to read the passage. Have a volunteer come to the front to begin reading, with everyone else following along in their own Bibles. Let the group know that anyone can shout "Switch," come to the front, and pick up where the other person left off. Ask students to look for natural breaks. Continue until the entire chapter has been read.

Break up into small groups with at least one adult leader in each group. Hand out the **The Greatest Gift** worksheets (page 47) and have your students complete them.

Application (10 minutes)

At this point bring the kids mentally back to the gift exchange. Have a few volunteers share what they felt were the best gifts and why. Then, wrap up this session with comments such as the following:

> **We've had fun sharing and rating our gifts, but let's think about God's incredibly, important gift. The gift of faith in Christ brings with it three powerful benefits:**
> ■ **Peace with God**
> ■ **Unlimited access to God's presence and friendship**
> ■ **A deep sense of hope and inner security that we experience as joy.**
> **What are you going to do with this gift? It's a great gift that includes everything we need to have a wonderful life. God's holding it out to you. What will you say to him?**

Hand out A **Thank-You Note to God** (page 49) and give them time to fill it out. Encourage them to share their responses with a family member or a good friend.

Go over the memory verse, hand out verse cards, restate the Big Idea, and refer to the poster.

End with a prayer time using only one-word prayers of thanksgiving.

Real faith brings peace with God.

Introduce your special guest, The Iceman (or Icewoman), who was frozen in a cave 3,000 years ago, was thawed by a volcanic eruption, and is just now learning about his modern surroundings. He's heard about Jesus but doesn't know anything about the gospel.

Have the Iceman explain about the culture he came from, how they sacrificed to their gods, and how they tried to live good lives—the more dramatic the better. Then the Iceman can ask the kids questions. (Before his performance you should prompt him about the details of the lesson so he can ask questions that will elicit the students' understanding of this chapter.)

Romans 5:1-21

The Greatest Gift

I. The key to understanding verses 1-11 is understanding verse 1:

> Therefore, since we have been justified through faith, we have peace with God through our Lord Jesus Christ.

Check the phrase that best summarizes verse 1:

❑ a. If I have faith, I have victory (total control) over sin.

❑ b. My faith is what makes me right before God.

❑ c. God accepts me because of how I serve him.

What's wrong with the other two choices?

2. What are the results of being justified through faith, and what does it mean to you?

Verses	Result	What It Means to Me
1		
2		
2-3		

3. Read verses 3-4. Think about what the Bible means when it refers to "suffering for Jesus." Rank the following statements from 1 (most closely matches the biblical meaning of suffering for Jesus) to 8 (furthest from the biblical meaning):

___ Being teased or ignored for carrying a Bible

___ Standing up for someone who's different

___ Staying at home instead of going out drinking

___ Being made fun of for wearing a Christian T-shirt

___ Being left out of a group of friends because you didn't party with them

___ Forgiving someone who hurt you

___ Feeling sad and broken-hearted for those who are spiritually lost

___ Being made fun of for starting a prayer group on campus

4. Based on verses 5-11, where does our hope come from? How do we get it?

5. Verse 15 says, "The gift is not like the trespass."

What's the gift?

What's the trespass?

What did the trespass buy?

What did the gift buy?

Romans 5:1-21

The Greatest Gift

Leader's Guide

1 Being justified through faith refers to our spiritual positions before God, but it doesn't affect the sin nature that resides in our physical bodies, so **a.** is false. Obedience and works don't save us, so **c.** is false, too. Our justification—a legal term meaning pardon from the consequences of sin—is based only on our faith, or trust, in Jesus Christ, so **b.** is the correct answer.

2 The three results of being justified through faith: peace with God, access to God, and hope and joy.

3 There may be some misunderstanding of this concept among your kids. Although some people believe that suffering means any opposition at all, there are those—including myself—who believe that Christian suffering is either oppression for living in a way that reflects our faith or the internal suffering we experience on behalf of those who are under sin's influence.

This question may jumpstart a discussion about experiencing suffering when we're arrogant and self-righteous and may deserve the suffering that comes our way versus experiencing suffering for loving others and walking humbly with Jesus. (Look up Matthew 6:5-8 and Colossians 4:5-6 for more discussion fuel.)

The last part of Question 3 is designed to help students walk through the process God uses to transform suffering into good. For any given statement ask, "How does your number one choice about suffering produce perseverance? How does that produce character? How does that produce hope?"

4 We have hope because God has given us the Holy Spirit. People have struggled for centuries to understand what Paul means in his references to Adam in verses 12-14, but over the years the general consensus has become that Adam's sin in the garden was representative of all of us.

Stott states, "If it is true that we sinned in and with Adam, it is yet more gloriously true that we died and rose again in and with Christ" (page 154).

5 ■ The gift is justification through faith.
■ The trespass is Adam's sin.
■ The trespass brought death to all.
■ The gift brings justification to all who have faith in Christ.

Romans 5:1-21

A THANK-YOU NOTE TO GOD

Thank You

Dear God,

Thanks for giving me peace with you. The best thing about it is . . .

Thanks for giving me access to you. It helps me to know . . .

Thanks for giving me hope and joy. When I think about these two things, I think . . .

Thanks for the gift of faith. I want to . . .

Love,

Romans 5:1-21

The Gift

Cast
Bob
Sue

Prop
A nicely wrapped gift

Bob: Hi, Sue. What's up?

Sue: *(carrying the gift)* Hi, Bob. Where are you going so fast? I was just on my way to your house.

Bob: *(interrupting Sue)* I'm kinda in a rush, Sue. I'm on my way to buy tickets for tonight's concert . . . $200 a piece . . . from a scalper. They're his last tickets, so I've gotta rush . . .

Sue: That's why I was coming over. I've got something for you.

Bob: Great! What's it for? It's not my birthday, I don't think. What is it?

Sue: It's just a really expensi . . . well, a gift to let you know that I think you're a great guy and I like you.

Bob: Cool! Okay, what'd you get me?

Sue: Well, you have to see for yourself.

Bob: Okay, great! *(starts to reach for the gift, and stops, thinking)* But, well, I'm in kind of a hurry, and, um, why don't you just tell me what it is and we'll get past all this suspense?

Sue: What suspense? I just want to give you this gift, but you need to take it and open it for it to mean anything to you.

Bob: What do you mean, "Mean anything to me"? I want your gift, and I appreciate that you like me, but, like I said, I'm in a real big hurry and I'm not sure if I've got time for this. All I want to know is what's in there? *(pointing to the package)*

Sue: It's a gift for you!

Bob: I know it's a gift for me, but I want to know what it is!

Sue: What's what?

Bob: That! *(pointing to the present)*

Sue: A gift for you!

Bob: Okay, okay. Thank you for the gift. I appreciate it. I really do. Now, all I want to know is: What is the gift?!

Sue: Why?

Bob: What do you mean, "Why?" Just because, okay? I don't know.

Sue: Don't you want it?

Bob: Well, sure. I mean, probably, but, well, um, it sorta depends on . . .

Sue: Depends on what?

Bob: Um, on, well . . . if it fits, or, well, you know . . .

Sue: Look, Bob, I have this gift for you because I like you, you're my friend, and you mean a lot to me. Do you want it or not?

Bob: Sure, okay, yes. Yes, I want the gift. *(reaches out his hand)*

Sue: Great, okay. Here you go . . . *(starts to hand him the gift, but thinks about it)* On second thought, it's not that big of a deal. Why don't you stop by tomorrow for it?

Bob: Thanks, Sue . . . sure, okay. Gotta run, see ya. . .

Sue: Wait!

Bob: What now?

Sue: Aren't you just a little bit curious?

Bob: Sure I am, but I've gotta go get those tickets. *(runs off stage)*

Sue: *(after Bob is gone)* Hope you enjoy the concert, if you get a ticket, that is. It would have been great if you could have gone with me and sat in the front row tonight. *(holds up the gift)* Here's your ticket! Maybe Kevin will want to go with me. Hmm . . . *(she walks off stage, opposite of Bob)*

— END —

SESSION FIVE

LIVING FOR CHRIST
Romans 6:1-23

BIG IDEA
Because you die only once, live for Christ now.

Overview

Paul doesn't wait for readers to raise objections to what he's presented up to this point (justification by faith through grace)—so he raises the objections himself.

By proposing—rhetorically—that we continue to rebel so that grace can increase, he sets the stage to reject what Bonhoeffer a half century ago called "cheap grace." Grace is never cheap, because Jesus Christ paid for it with his life. (Be prepared to answer—or at least discuss—what some students who disagree with Bonhoeffer may point out: that grace, by definition, is most certainly cheap, in that it's free.) When Paul connects the new life believers have (through faith) to the death and resurrection of Jesus, Paul affirms that we're no longer under the judgment of sin—although he does argue that we remain under the influence and power of sin if we choose to live by the sin nature still operating within us. The decision to live by faith is a choice.

An important piece of Paul's argument is noteworthy: "Now if we died with Christ, we believe that we will also live with him" (verse 8), soon followed by "The death he died, he died to sin once for all" (verse 10). Just as Jesus died only once (notice the past tense in both verses), we die only once, with Christ. Paul's emphasis is not on the one-time event of death to sin, but on recognizing that we now are alive in Christ.

In other words, because much Christian teaching in this century has focused on what we're to avoid, we tend to overlook what we're called to embrace—our life in Christ.

This passage also contains important teaching on baptism (verses 3-4). Because interpretations of what Paul meant vary so much, be sure you have a good understanding of your church's position; consult your church

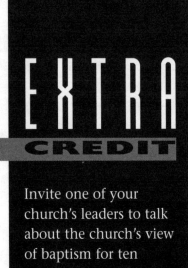

leadership before teaching this session, if necessary.

Many theologians interpret this teaching as a picture of salvation. To be baptized in Jesus' name is to be identified through faith with Jesus' death on the cross and his resurrection. It's a picture of our willingness to put our own selfishness to death, just as Jesus died for us. The resurrection of Jesus reflects the new life we have when we believe in him. Verse 5 is a summary of this interpretation,

> If we have been united with him like this
> in his death, we will certainly also be
> united with him in his resurrection.

The second half of the chapter is very practical. The war has been won ("anyone who has died has been freed from sin," verse 7), yet we still have to live the new life we have in Christ ("now offer them [your bodies] in slavery to righteousness leading to holiness," verse 19).

We battle the influence of the sinful nature, but it no longer reigns over us. (For more on this, read Galatians 2, especially verse 20).

Before the Meeting

1. Get the **Living for Christ** worksheet (page 55) and its **Leader's Guide** (page 56) to your small-group leaders a week before the lesson.
2. Write this session's **Big Idea** on a whiteboard, bulletin board, poster, overhead transparency, or wherever it can catch students' eyes during the teaching session. Ideally, after the meeting add this Big Idea to a cumulative list somewhere in the room (perhaps on an empty wall) so your group can track what they've studied in Romans. If you don't have the wall space, use the master on page 115 to make a transparency to project during your review time at the beginning of each session; reveal only the Big Ideas you've studied to date.
3. Using the reproducible master on page 57, make enough **Live for God cards** to give one to each student. (You may want to make copies for weekly use, or for other groups.)
4. Photocopy enough copies of the **Instruments of Righteousness Bingo** sheet (page 58) for every student.
5. Have newspapers, scissors, posterboard, and glue ready to distribute as soon as **Instruments of Righteousness Bingo** is over.
6. Recruit a church leader to speak briefly about your church's position on baptism if you're using this option.

Opening (15 minutes)

Hand out **Instruments of Righteousness Bingo** sheet (page 58) and pens. Direct your teens to do the activities that will satisfy any horizontal, vertical, or diagonal row for a bingo. The person served should initial the square. If you want the game to last a little longer, have the kids complete two bingos.

As a variation, you can divide your students into smaller groups and only let them approach others in their own small group. There are two ways to determine winners:

- The first five finishers win a prize
- All those that get a bingo within the predetermined time limit win a prize

Hand out the prizes when the game is over.

Scripture (30 minutes)

Review the past four **Big Ideas** and display the posters as you have in the past.

Break up into groups of six students or less, with at least one adult leader for each group. Distribute scissors, posterboard, glue or tape, and a stack of newspapers to each group. Give the following instructions:

- **Take the first ten minutes to read Romans 6:1-23.**
- **Cut out as many headlines as the group can find that communicate some aspect of the passage.**
- **Glue the headlines to their posterboard.**

When the time is up, have groups share their posterboards with each other.

Now, distribute the **Living for Christ** worksheet (page 55) and send the students back to their groups to complete them.

Application (15 minutes)

After the groups finish the worksheet, bring everyone back together. Present the memory verse, hand out the verse cards, restate the lesson's **Big Idea**, and refer to the poster.

Hand out one **Live for God card** to each student (page 57). Prime the pump by brainstorming several ways they can live for God this week. Give them a few minutes to write down an original or group idea that they would be willing to do during the upcoming week. Encourage them to keep the card with them.

Check with your students at the next meeting to see how well they followed through.

Close by having leaders pray that the students will keep their personal commitments to live for God during the week.

Break the class into two teams to play Romans Pictionary. Here's how to play: each team chooses ten words or concepts from Romans 6 that the opposing team has to draw. The team that is drawing first sends one player to look at the first word. He or she has fifteen seconds to plan the drawing, and then draws pictures to get teammates to guess the word. Drawing numbers, letters, and symbols are big no-no's; so are verbal clues and gestures. The team has one minute to guess the answer. Award points for the correct answer. Alternate play. Reward the team with the most points.

LIVING FOR CHRIST

1. In your own words, what's Paul arguing against as he opens this chapter?

2. There are many different views about what Paul meant when he wrote about baptism in verses 3-4. Read verses 3-6. What is Paul's point in verses 5-6?

With the previous question in mind, what does being "baptized into Christ Jesus" mean?

3. Read verse 6 and note Paul's reference to the body of sin. By the context we know he wasn't referring to physical bodies. What do you think he's referring to? Explain why you think so.

4. According to verses 5-11, how many times can someone die to sin?

Now read Galatians 2:20, which was also written by Paul. Restate what he says there in your own words:

5. Look carefully at verses 15-23. Circle the number that best represents each statement.

	True	Sorta true	I dunno	Sorta false	False
a. My "body of sin" is totally destroyed	1	2	3	4	5
b. Sin no longer has any power to tempt me	1	2	3	4	5
c. I'm no longer a slave to sin, but sin still has influence	1	2	3	4	5
d. Being dead to sin is the legal, descriptive truth, but I still struggle with sin	1	2	3	4	5

Use verses from Romans 6 to support the truth of statements you ranked 1 or 2.

Romans 6:1-23

LIVING FOR CHRIST

1 By the way Paul begins his argument, it's as if you can hear two different voices responding in two different ways to the letter so far. The first one says, "The more we sin, the more God forgives us—so we might as well have a good time." The second one says, "Grace is important, but God still wants us to work!" Paul's argument takes on both of these objections.

2 This area must be taught and discussed from the perspective of your church's own tradition and theology. This is a good point at which to have the church leader make a presentation (see **Extra Credit**, page 52).

3 Most people believe the body of sin is the same things as our fallen, sinful nature.

4 It may seem obvious to ask, "How many times can you die to sin?" yet Christians often talk about the answer to this question as if we must die over and over again to the sinful nature.

　　The best way to describe the Bible's teaching on this is to say we die one time to the selfish nature, and we now live for Christ, empowered by the Holy Spirit. We battle the effects of the old self, but in reality, once it's been put to death, it no longer controls us. If your students are confused by this, look at Galatians 2:20 with them. In Christ, we're now alive with Jesus living inside of us.

5 The following answers are based on Romans 6:15-23:
 a. No, the body of sin is not totally destroyed, but its ultimate power over us is gone. The process of trusting Jesus more and obeying him better is called sanctification.
 b. Big-time false. Even the most mature believers are still learning to live under the control of the Spirit.
 c. Now that we're in Christ, we have a choice: trusting God, which leads to reward, or trusting our selfish sin nature, which leads to destruction. The process of learning to make the right choice is a lifelong process for all Christians.
 d. Since we're in Christ, God has declared us holy. Even though we will always struggle against the influence of the sin nature, we can be confident that God will help us in our struggles.

Romans 6:1-23
LIVE FOR GOD CARDS

Because I live for God now, this week I will—	Because I live for God now, this week I will—
Because I live for God now, this week I will—	Because I live for God now, this week I will—
Because I live for God now, this week I will—	Because I live for God now, this week I will—
Because I live for God now, this week I will—	Because I live for God now, this week I will—

Romans 6:1-23

INSTRUMENTS OF RIGHTEOUSNESS BINGO

Offer yourselves to God, as those who have been brought from death to life; and offer the parts of your body to him as instruments of righteousness. Romans 6:13

Pick up someone and gently carry them 10 feet	Do your best 30-second dance for someone	Find someone you don't know (or whom you know the least), and introduce him or her to someone *they* don't know very well	Find someone who looks like they're discouraged and whisper something nice to them	Find someone to celebrate. Get a party horn from a leader, blow it, and march around the person yelling, "Celebrate (their name)!" 20 times
Find someone who looks tired and give them a 30-second back rub	Find someone with laced shoes; untie and re-tie the laces	Make a paper airplane that actually flies; give it to someone else	Whistle a happy tune for one minute for someone	Blow up a balloon and give it to someone who has a birthday within two months of today
Sing the first verse of an encouraging song to someone	Make up a poem and recite it to someone	FREE SPACE	Tell someone about your best friend in elementary school for one minute	Serve as someone's personal bodyguard for one minute
Give someone a dollar	Find out someone's favorite color and give them something that's yours to give in that color	Sing someone their favorite song	Play Rock, Paper, Scissors with someone until one of you has won 15 times	Find the happiest person you see, ask him or her to tell you why he or she is so happy — and listen to the answer
Tell someone 10 wonderful character and/or physical traits they possess	Give someone a handshake, a high-five, and a standing ovation	Ask someone five questions, and after they answer them, repeat their answers back to them	Draw a work of art for another person and give it to them	Give someone lighter than you a piggy-back ride for 20 feet

SESSION SIX

THE SIN STRUGGLE
Romans 7:1-25

BIG IDEA
Sin is the battle, but the war has been won.

Overview

In the first of this chapter's two distinct sections, Paul finishes up his discussion about sin and the law with an illustration from marriage.

The problem for the modern reader is understanding the first-century context of Paul's remarks about marriage. Today a divorced woman is generally not considered an adulteress if she marries another man while her ex-husband is still alive, but in Paul's culture a divorced woman was forbidden to remarry. With this understanding, Paul's illustration of how death changes the rules makes sense.

(Although he continues with this theme until verse 13, verse 6 is an excellent summary of the last several chapters: "But now, by dying to what once bound us, we have been released from the law so that we serve in the new way of the Spirit, and not in the old way of the written code.")

The second section of this chapter, which begins with verse 14, may be the most hotly debated passage in the entire book of Romans. The problem may be that what he writes doesn't appear to fit with the message of the book: "I have the desire to do what is good, but I cannot carry it out" is Paul's cry in verse 18, even though he's confident about his righteousness in Christ in the rest of the letter.

As you read through this section, consider that perhaps Paul is speaking on behalf of those he's trying to convince. It's plausible that the apostle is speaking from the perspective of the believer who loves Jesus Christ—and who is under grace—but who is still trying to meet the demands of the law in his or her own strength.

On the other hand, others argue, Paul is only articulating the human dilemma: even as a man made righteous by Christ, he yet doesn't seem to be able to live up to his calling like he wants to.

In any case, Paul is masterful in setting up the reader to learn how to live by faith and not by works in the next few chapters.

MATERIALS NEEDED

- TV, VCR, and the video *The Princess Bride* (1987, PG)
- Whiteboard and markers
- A variety of magazines (mainstream, not Christian)
- A few pairs of scissors and rolls of Scotch tape, and posterboard
- Copies of **The War Has Been Won!** (page 63)
- Homemade videotape of a variety of TV commercials (optional; see **For the Younger Set**, page 61)
- Videotape of a student who's graduated from your group reading Romans 7
- Copies of **Contract with God** (page 65)
- Soloist to sing "Amazing Grace" (or play the song on tape or CD)
- This session's **Big Idea** written on a whiteboard, poster, etc.
- Bibles and pencils (or pens) for all students and adults
- Scripture memory verse cards (page 116)

Before the Meeting

1. Arrange to have a former student (older than the students in your group) read Romans 7:1-25 on video. Make sure the quality of the video is good before you show it to the students.

2. Record some TV commercials as described on page 61 if you elect to pursue **For the Younger Set** option.

3. Preview the video clip from *The Princess Bride* to determine its suitability for your group. By the VCR counter, the segment is 20:90 to 23:76 That's the scene in which the hero, Wesley, challenges the evil kidnapper to a battle of wits over a cup of poison. To cue the video by the VCR counter, set the counter on 00:00 when the first credit appears. Then fast-forward to 20:90. Cue up the video and adjust the sound before students arrive.

   Consider setting up a time to watch the entire movie a week or so before the session; it'll enhance the impact of the scene on your teens during the teaching session.

4. Get the **War Has Been Won!** (page 63) and its **Leader's Guide** (page 64) to your small-group leaders a week before the lesson.

5. Write this session's Big Idea on a whiteboard, bulletin board, poster, overhead transparency, or wherever it can catch students' eyes during the teaching session. Ideally, after the meeting add this Big Idea to a cumulative list somewhere in the room (perhaps on an empty wall) so your group can track what they've studied in Romans. If you don't have the wall space, use the master on page 115 to make a transparency to project during your review time at the beginning of each session; reveal only the Big Ideas you've studied to date.

6. Have the magazines, scissors, posterboard, and tape ready to hand out as soon as you finish discussing temptations. Have enough supplies so that each small group has their own.

7. Recruit a soloist to sing "Amazing Grace" a cappella at the end of the lesson. If this is impossible, locate a tape or CD version to play.

Opening (10 minutes)

Show the *Princess Bride* episode.

As a group, brainstorm what struggles typical young people face today, listing them on a whiteboard. Shortly after they get rolling, guide the discussion—if it's not already there—to temptations Christian students face.

To select the top five temptations, give each student three votes. They may vote for one temptation with three votes, three different temptations at one vote each, or any combination that totals three. Students can vote by holding up the number of fingers they want to vote as each temptation is announced. Keep a running record of votes on the board.

When you're finished, make a new list of the top five.

Activity: Posters (15 minutes)

Transition by stating something along these lines:

A major source of temptation is the huge number of unhealthy messages we're bombarded with every day through the media. The modern-day version of the American Dream is that, with enough money and effort, we can do or have anything we want. If we can do or have anything we want, we will be happy and fulfilled.

Break into small groups of five or fewer students with an adult leader in each. Hand each group a few magazines, scissors, posterboard, and tape.

Give them five minutes to find an advertisement that tempts believers to trust themselves for fulfillment in life, not Jesus. Cut it out, tape it to the poster, and write a few words as a caption. If there's enough time, add one or two more.

After every group has at least one, have a volunteer from each group come to the front to share what they found.

After all the groups have shared, give them an opportunity to reflect on their findings. Ask questions like—

■ **What did you learn by doing this?**
■ **What thoughts will you take home with you?**

When the discussion is finished, read this quote from Donald McCullough's book, *Waking from the American Dream* (InterVarsity Press, 1988):

We live in a culture that tells us our dreams can be realized with enough hard work and positive thinking. But at one time or another, we wake up to reality. We learn, often with great pain, that we can't always have what we desperately want. Perhaps a marriage leaves us lonelier than we thought possible, or a single life feels like an inescapable prison, or sexual drives remain frustrated, or vocational advancement has been blocked, or health evades us, or God seems to have locked Himself in an unresponsive heaven—disappointment comes in a variety of ways, and it can send us straight into the pit.

Follow up with a comment such as—

We're constantly tempted to make our own path, but God says there's only one way. Let's look at the Bible to see what it is.

for the **YOUNGER SET**

Show some TV commercials you've prerecorded that have power to influence students' attitudes and actions about sex, clothes, self-image, or money. Discuss what each commercial communicates about trusting God for our fulfillment or joy in life.

MEMORY VERSE

Romans 7:4

So, my brothers, you also died to the law through the body of Christ, that you might belong to another, to him who was raised from the dead, in order that we might bear fruit to God.

▼▼▼▼▼▼▼

Scripture (25 minutes)

Review the Big Ideas and display the posters as before.

Show the video of the former student reading Romans 7:1-25 while everyone follows along in their own Bibles.

Break into groups of five or fewer students, each with at least one adult leader. Have them complete **The War Has Been Won!** (page 63).

Application (10 minutes)

After bringing the class back together, present the memory verse and hand out the verse cards. Review the Big Idea and refer to the poster.

Distribute the **Contract with God** handout (page 65) and give students a few minutes to complete it.

As a closing prayer, have the soloist sing "Amazing Grace" a capella, or play a recorded version of the song.

Romans 7:1-25
THE WAR HAS BEEN WON!

1. Put Paul's argument from verses 1-3 into your own words. (In Paul's culture, divorced women were not allowed to remarry until their ex-husbands died)

2. In verse 4 Paul writes, "You also died to the law through the body of Christ." Sometimes the phrase "the body of Christ" refers to the church, but in this passage he means the actual death of Jesus. When we acknowledge that Jesus died in our place—that we're the ones who should have been punished because of our sin, and that Jesus hadn't done anything wrong—then we live by the Spirit, not under the law.

With this in mind, read verses 4-6 and circle the most accurate response:

Do I believe that Jesus died for me?	Yes	I'm not sure	No
Have I stopped living by the law?	Yes	I'm not sure	No
Do I belong to Christ?	Yes	I'm not sure	No

How do these questions make you feel? Why?

3. We may delight in God's law, but we can't fulfill it on our own. The weakness of the law is that it can't make us do it. It doesn't give us any power. We only get the power for victory from the Spirit of God.

Put an X to show how you are doing:

Struggling on my own ←————→ Family ←————→ **Responding to the Spirit**
←————→ School ←————→
←————→ Social life ←————→
←————→ Faith ←————→
←————→ Thought life ←————→

4. Review your answers to Question 3. What's your greatest struggle right now? (Use code if you want to keep it private.)

Read Romans 7:24-25. How can Jesus rescue you from your struggle?

Romans 7:1-25
THE WAR HAS BEEN WON!
LEADER'S GUIDE

Students should complete the worksheet individually. After everyone is finished, go through each question as a group.

1 According to the interpretation of Jewish law during Paul's era, a woman was allowed to be married only one time as long as her husband was alive, even if she got divorced. (Most modern Jewish commentators reject this interpretation.) To Paul's audience it was a convincing illustration.

2 This passage presents some difficult concepts. The kids' answers will give you a good idea of how much they understand. The first question reflects the idea that Jesus' death is for every individual. The second deals with what keeps us from God (the subject of recent lessons). The third question asks for the student's personal response.

3 and 4 Romans 7 is personally applied in these two questions. If students are reluctant to share what they wrote, ask them more general questions:

- How difficult was it to respond to these questions?
- What's the difference between struggling on my own and responding to the Spirit?
- How can Jesus Christ rescue us from our struggles?

Romans 7:1-25

CONTRACT WITH GOD

The one thing I will do this week to let God change me from the inside out:

Furthermore, I'll talk with _____ this week to help me with this contract.
(name)

I'll contact this person no later than: _____
(date)

I'll ask him/her to:

Signature _____ Date _____

SESSION SEVEN

MORE THAN CONQUERORS
Romans 8:1-39

BIG IDEA
In Christ we are more than conquerors.

MATERIALS
NEEDED

- Pens, 3 x 5 cards, tape (masking or clear), markers
- A prize or two for the **Opening** game (page 68)
- Whiteboard and markers
- Blow Pops (optional; see **For the Younger Set**, page 69)
- Copies of **More Than Conquerors!** (page 71)
- Copies of **Grace Graph** (page 73)
- This session's **Big Idea** written on a whiteboard, poster, etc.
- Bibles and pencils (or pens) for all students and adults
- Scripture memory verse cards (page 116)

Overview

Romans 8 is one of the classic chapters of encouragement in the Bible. Paul begins with a powerful summary of faith in Christ: "Therefore, there is now no condemnation for those who are in Christ Jesus." The he explains how grace affects our battle with sin. Verses 3-17 define the difference between a believer and a nonbeliever: nonbelievers don't have the Spirit of Christ; believers do. His description—in verses 9-10—is the reason some refer to a profession of faith as "inviting Christ into my life."

However you interpret this concept, Paul's description and meaning are clear. The Spirit lives in those who are justified through faith, and there are some who don't possess the Spirit.

Those who have the Spirit are God's children, complete with a father-child relationship with God (a healthy one, an intimate one). We call him Daddy, Abba.

Because of our intimate relationship with him, we will also have a part in Christ's sufferings.

The present sufferings that Paul talks about in verses 18-25 have received a great deal of attention as well as theological conjecture. The **Leader's Guide** (page 72) discusses different interpretations of suffering for Jesus, but the passage doesn't give us much direct information to draw a firm conclusion.

Verses 26 and 27 contain an incredible truth that is easy to gloss over, but it's worth giving attention to: God the Holy Spirit prays for us.

How is this possible? What does this mean? Even though we can only guess at the answers, the fact remains that God is so concerned about us that the provision of prayer is covered personally within the heart of God.

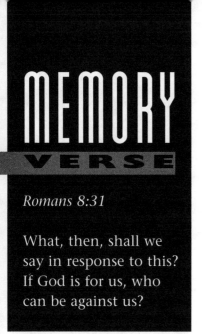

MEMORY VERSE

Romans 8:31

What, then, shall we say in response to this? If God is for us, who can be against us?

▼▼▼▼▼▼▼▼

Paul closes the chapter with a head of steam. Verse 31 appears to be the focal point of the text: "If God is for us, who can be against us?" Paul is convinced that God's love can penetrate any obstacle that attempts to block it.

Before the Meeting

1. Get the **More Than Conquerors!** worksheet (page 71) and its **Leader's Guide** (page 72) to your small-group leaders a week before the lesson.

2. Write this session's **Big Idea** on a whiteboard, bulletin board, poster, overhead transparency, or wherever it can catch students' eyes during the teaching session. Ideally, after the meeting add this Big Idea to a cumulative list somewhere in the room (perhaps on an empty wall) so your group can track what they've studied in Romans. If you don't have the wall space, use the master on page 115 to make a transparency to project during your review time at the beginning of each session; reveal only the Big Ideas you've studied to date.

3. Write the names of sports on 3 x 5 cards until you have one for each student—the more unusual, the better (polo, curling, badminton, steeplechase, cricket, ping pong, etc.) Tape one card to the underside of each chair.

4. Recruit adult leaders to read Romans 8 popcorn style (see **Scripture**, page 69).

Opening (10 minutes)

Open this session by playing Guess the Fan. Have your students sit on the chairs with the cards taped underneath. Explain the game like this:

Thanks to the wonders of modern technology, each of you is now a rabid sports fan, whether you know or not. In a minute, you will receive a card that will tell you the name of the sport you love. As soon as you have gotten your card, the game begins. Follow these rules:

■ **There are two objects to the game: (1) keep your own sport a secret as long as possible, and (2) guess the sports of as many other people as possible.**

■ **When the game begins, go to anyone you want and ask them yes or no questions about their sport. You can ask each player up to five questions.**

■ **When you think you know someone's sport, you can guess. If you're right, have them write your name on their card. Keep trying to guess other people's sports. If you're wrong, you can't ask that person any more questions at any time.**

Play Blow Pop Trivia. Prepare a list of trivia questions, some related to the Big Ideas covered so far and others that are of general interest to your students (sports, events at school, community activities, etc.).

After reading the trivia question, the first student to silently raise his or her hand is chosen. If the student answers correctly, he or she is awarded a Blow Pop and can't answer any more questions. If kids don't answer correctly, they're still in the game. Anyone who blurts out an answer is disqualified.

Display the Big Ideas posters as the corresponding question is correctly answered.

Don't use the trivia questions for the Big Ideas in order:

LESSON	QUESTIONS	ANSWERS
1	What gives us confidence?	God is at work in us
2	What's the way out of our rebellion against God?	Faith
3	_____ is my job, changing me is God's.	Faith or trust or belief
4	Real faith brings _____.	Peace with God
5	How often are we supposed to die to our sinful nature?	Only once (now we live for God)
6	Sin is a battle, but _____.	The war has been won

Start the game and let them go at it for five minutes. Tally the results and award prizes to the person who correctly guessed the most sports.

Have your kids brainstorm the characteristics of an enthusiastic fan. List these on your whiteboard.

Scripture (30 minutes)

Review the last six **Big Ideas** and display the posters as previously done.

Students should open their Bibles to Romans 8 and follow along with the adult leaders reading popcorn style. One stands and reads a few verses, then someone else pops up and reads several more. Continue in this manner until the passage has been read. Designate in advance who will read which verses so they can practice reading before the session.

Divide students into small groups with at least one adult leader per group to complete the **More Than Conquers!** handout (page 71).

Application (20 minutes)

Gather the students together to introduce the memory verse and hand out verse cards.

Review the Big Idea and refer to the poster. Transition into the application activity by asking the kids how deeply they let this truth sink into them.

Hand out the **Grace Graph** (page 73) worksheet and ask the kids to complete everything but the prescription.

When they're finished, brainstorm some specific ideas for improving scores. Write them all on the board. Give kids a chance to choose an idea that would remedy their self-diagnoses and write it as their prescriptions along with three specific action steps they can take to follow through on their prescriptions. Give them some examples like talking to a friend or family member to hold him or her accountable or writing down one friend to ask for forgiveness.

Close with prayer for each other to follow through on prescription plans this week.

More Than Conquerors!

1. Verses 1-4 are a summary of the previous seven chapters. In the space below, draw a picture that reflects what these verses are about. You can add a caption if you want.

2. What name does Paul use for the Holy Spirit in each of the following verses?
Verse 4

Verse 9 (three names)

Verse 11

Verse 14

What reason is there for using all of these names?

3. What type of person is controlled by the Spirit?

What type of person is controlled by the sinful nature?

Does everyone have the Spirit? (Check one)
❏ Yes   ❏No
Why or why not?

4. What are three examples of creation groaning in "its bondage to decay"? (for example, earthquakes)

1.

2.

3.

5. Read verses 31-39. What does "God is for you" mean to you?

6. Finish the following sentence: In Christ, I'm more than a conqueror because . . .

Romans 8:1-39
More than Conquerors!
LEADER'S GUIDE

Because the Big Idea—"In Christ, we're more than conquerors!"—is a shout of victory, this lesson is intended to be a crescendo of powerful encouragement.

1 This is your chance to make sure that the students are ready to make the leap from the first half of Romans to the second half. If you have new students or if any of the kids have a hard time remembering what past lessons have been about, take a few minutes to review. Let students respond to Question 1 individually and then share their drawings if they want to. After you have finished with this question, the kids can complete the rest of the worksheet on their own.

2 Here are the names for the Holy Spirit:

VERSE	NAME
4	The Spirit
9	The Spirit, The Spirit of God, The Spirit of Christ
11	The Spirit
14	The Spirit of God

All three are different names for the same Spirit—the Holy Spirit who is the third person of the Trinity. Although the doctrine of the Trinity wasn't developed yet, the idea of the Trinity was clearly in Paul's mind.

3 According to the passage, those who have the Spirit living in them are controlled by the Spirit and are God's children. Conversely, people who don't have the Spirit are controlled by their sinful natures.
Though various church traditions differ on the exact meaning of this passage, Paul makes a clear-cut distinction between those who have the Spirit and those who don't. Most of historic Christianity has affirmed that those who believe in Jesus Christ through faith are given the gift of the indwelling Holy Spirit.

4 Paul reveals that all of creation is groaning—it's breaking down—until Jesus returns. But he also encourages us with the hope that some day God will make everything new. While we're waiting, God is personally looking after us: God the Holy Spirit constantly intercedes with God the Father on our behalf (verses 26-27).

5 Read verses 31-39. What does "God is for you" mean to you? If your teens are stuck, ask them, "How do you need God to be for you? In what area do you feel like you need a cheering fan?" Help the kids see how they have nothing to fear because of the love God has for us.

6 Have the students finish the sentence and share their answers with their groups.

Romans 8:1-39

Grace Graph

Place an X on the lines where you are. Include a brief explanation in the space below each.

Temperature

I'm feverish for Jesus!

90° ⟷ 108°

Head

Jesus is my greatest fan!

No way! ⟷ Absolutely!

Heart

I'm experiencing God's love in my life!

Hardly ever ⟷ Regularly

Hands

I obey God because he loves me!

Hardly ever ⟷ Regularly

General health

I'm a conqueror!

Not me! ⟷ Convinced!

Diagnosis: (What's my condition?)

Prescription: (What can I do this week to improve my condition?)

SESSION EIGHT

SUPPORTED BY THE ROOT
Romans 9:1-11:36

BIG IDEA
We do not support the root—the root supports us.

MATERIALS NEEDED

- Sheets of paper
- Whiteboard and markers
- Three prizes for **Opening** game (page 76)
- Copies of **Stuck to the Vine!** (page 79)
- Potted plant with a complex root ball (see **Before the Meeting**, page 76, point 3)
- This session's **Big Idea** written on a whiteboard, poster, etc.
- Bibles and pencils (or pens) for all students and adults
- Scripture memory verse cards (page 116)

Overview

Paul agonized over the fate of the Israelites, those who had always considered themselves God's favored ones because of their careful adherence to the law. Although Paul deeply loved the people of his own race, he was compelled to present the truth God had passed on to him by the Holy Spirit (notice the painstaking detail with which he explains these truths).

As Paul explains it, the true family of Israel isn't formed by birth but by faith.

> *For not all who are descended from Israel are Israel (9:6).*

The death and resurrection of Jesus changed our *understanding* of the promise—not the promise itself—made to Abraham about his children.

> *It is not the natural children who are God's children, but it is the children of the promise who are regarded as Abraham's offspring (9:8).*

Anticipating a strong reaction to this teaching (which has continued to this day), Paul goes on to extend a very limited and noncomprehensive presentation of divine election.

> *God has mercy on whom he wants to have mercy, and he hardens whom he wants to harden (9:18).*

And he doesn't stop there. In the next breath, Paul deals out this blunt advice to those who think this is divine injustice:

> *But who are you, O man, to talk back to God? (9:20)*

One of Paul's reasons for writing this letter was to explain God's decision to bring salvation to the Gentiles as well as to the Jews. This was hard for Jews to swallow, yet Paul affirms God's right to have mercy on whomever he chooses.

Those with hard opinions about divine election often point to Romans 9 or Romans 10—the former for strong evidence for predestination (God's decision about who will be saved and who will not be—see 9:16-22), and Romans 10 to support free will and human responsibility (verses 9-15).

Others interpret Paul's comments to mean that Israel and the Gentiles are entities (see 10:16-21, and chapter 11). He wasn't defining or attempting to clarify the complexity and mystery of the free will-predestination paradox.

When Paul writes in Romans 11:26 that all Israel will be saved, he is wrapping up the first eleven chapters of the book by affirming that—according to one common interpretation—all those who are justified by faith in Jesus Christ's death and resurrection will be saved, whether Jew or Gentile. Others hold that everyone who is of Jewish decent *biologically* will somehow come to faith in Christ.

In any event, chapters 9-11 stand together (that's why this lesson covers all three) if we're to accurately understand Paul's message: we're saved by faith, not by heritage, culture, or human effort.

Before the Meeting

1. Get the **Stuck to the Vine!** worksheet (page 79) and its **Leader's Guide** (page 80) to your small-group leaders a week before the lesson.

2. Write this session's **Big Idea** on a whiteboard, bulletin board, poster, overhead transparency, or wherever it can catch students' eyes during the teaching session. Ideally, after the meeting add this Big Idea to a cumulative list somewhere in the room (perhaps on an empty wall) so your group can track what they've studied in Romans. If you don't have the wall space, use the master on page 115 to make a transparency to project during your review time at the beginning of each session; reveal only the Big Ideas you've studied to date.

3. Get a potted plant that has a complex root ball that takes up more volume than the top of the plant. (Any greenhouse or gardening store can help you.)

4. Recruit a student to practice and read John 15:1-8.

Opening (5 minutes)

Play the game Do You Have What I Have? Here's how it's played: hand out paper and pens. Have each student team up with another teen that he or she doesn't know very well (if possible) to generate a list of all of the unusual things that they both have or own. Both kids need to write a copy of the list.

Give examples of what's not really all that unusual, like a bed or a desk. Then list some relatively unusual things that could work, like an electric guitar or pet lizard.

After a few minutes, everyone must find a new partner and continue listing unusual things that the new teammates have in common, but the new rule is that they can't repeat anything on the list they already have.

After switching four or five times, ask everyone to sit down and total the number of items on their lists. Have everyone with two or more items stand up. Begin screening for the longest list by having kids with less than four sit down, then six or less. Repeat the process until you have three people left. Let each one read his or her list. The crowd can boo if an item is too ordinary.

Award prizes to the three with the longest lists.

Scripture (25 minutes)

Review all of the previous **Big Ideas** and display the posters.
Break into five groups with at least one adult leader each and assign the following sections.

GROUP	PASSAGE
1	Romans 9:1-18
2	Romans 9:19-33
3	Romans 10:1-21
4	Romans 11:1-21
5	Romans 11:22-36

After the group reads its portion any way it chooses, the kids must decide together on a key (summary) verse and write it on a blank piece of paper (which you can hand out along with pens and the **Stuck to the Vine!** worksheets (page 79) while they're reading). Allow five minutes to complete this part.

After bringing everyone back together, have one volunteer from each group present their key verse. Everyone should write down all the references to the key verses and a summary of what the verse says.

Return to the small groups to complete **Stuck to the Vine!**

Activity: Object lesson (10 minutes)

Bring everyone back together. Display a potted plant—still in the pot—whose root ball is larger or more expansive than the plant is above the surface of the dirt. Ask the students to describe what they see. Then pull the plant out of the pot and show them the relatively large root ball. Talk for a few minutes about the function of the roots—how they channel nutrients and water up to the plant, how they provide the physical support.

Have a volunteer read Romans 11:17-24 to the group. Ask—
What relationships can you see between the plant—both root ball and stalk—and the passage we just heard?

Ideas that can be included: the roots go widely or deeply into the soil the way our faith is deep and rich; there are many branches just like there are many believers (some Jewish, some Gentile); the roots support the branches as God supports us.

MEMORY VERSE

Romans 11:33

Oh, the depth of the riches of the wisdom and knowledge of God! How unsearchable his judgments, and his paths beyond tracing out!

▼ ▼ ▼ ▼ ▼ ▼ ▼

Application (20 minutes)

Ask a volunteer to read John 15:1-8.

Brainstorm how a plant's leaves need the stem and the roots to be healthy. Write all the ideas in a list on the left side of the whiteboard. On the right side of the board, write down how each of these ideas correlates to the needs we have for our stem (who is Jesus) and roots. For instance, a plant needs a stem and roots to be stable and not fall over—we need Jesus and the body of Christ to keep us stable and standing tall.

Introduce the memory verse, hand out the verse cards, review the Big Idea, and refer to the poster.

To close in prayer, have the leader name a topic that students can pray about. Periodically another topic can be announced. Possible topics: parents, other family members, pastors, school teachers, and school administrators.

Romans 9:1-11:36
Stuck to the Vine!

1. Write down the key verse each group came up with, and summarize that verse in your own words.

PASSAGE	KEY VERSE	MY VERSION
9:1-18		
9:18-33		
10:1-21		
11:1-21		
11:22-36		

2. Romans 9:18 states, "He [God] hardens whom he wants to harden." Although this passage may seem disturbing, there's no example in Scripture of God hardening the heart of anyone against his or her will. They all were rebelling against the Lord. Many people believe that God's hardening is the natural result of a stubborn and rebellious heart. Jot down a specific way you might be hardening your heart in one or two of following areas:

Family life

Social life

School life

Thought life

Faith

3. Read 11:17-24. What does this mean when a real plant has grafted branches?

Read John 15:1-8. Complete the following sentence:

_____ am the vine, _____ are the branches.

According to Romans 11:22, how do we remain connected to the vine?
What does this mean?

Who are the wild (natural) branches? ❏ Gentiles ❏ Jews
Who are the grafted in (cultivated) branches? ❏ Gentiles ❏ Jews

4. The root for both Jewish and Gentile believers is the same. God has been working through Israel to bring the gospel to all people. Romans 11:18 says, "Do not boast over those branches."
To whom is Paul talking?

What does he mean?

Why would anyone boast?

Stuck to the Vine!
L E A D E R ' S   G U I D E

1 Discuss all five key verses and student summaries. Make sure everyone in your group has written them down. After Question 1 students can complete the worksheet on their own.

2 The purpose of this question is to get students to see that a hard heart is first generated within so they can't blame God. If the issue causes a problem for your group, go back to Romans 1:24-28. The phrase "He [God] gave them over to—" is frequently used there. Psalm 95:7-11 is quoted in Hebrews 3:7-13: The antidote to a hardened heart is to "encourage one another daily" (verse 13).

3 Grafting is the process of tying a branch (not an original part of the plant) to a vine until they grow together so that the new branch functions as a living part of the vine.

   According to John 15, Jesus is the vine; we (believers in Christ) are the branches. According to Romans 11:22, the way we stay connected to the vine is by continuing in his kindness. This means that we must be willing to trust him and rely on him the best we can for everything (see John 15:5). Jews are the wild branches and Gentiles are grafted.

4 The Gentile Christians may have been saying that the Jews' history, the faith of Israel, didn't really matter. Paul is very strong in his response:

   "You do not support the root [the faith and history and writings of Israel]; but the root supports you" (verse 18).

Are we any different? Very few modern Christians even begin to recognize how our faith and the faith of the Jews are connected to the same vine. We must renew our respect for the race through which God chose to reveal his great love for us all.

SESSION NINE

LIVING SACRIFICE
Romans 12:1-21

BIG IDEA
We express our love for God by sacrificially loving others.

Overview

A much-cited and much-loved chapter, Romans 12 brings together the beauty and simplicity of the gospel lived out. It's not a legalistic set of rules to obey or standards to live up to. This warm, gentle chapter is a window into the kind of life the righteousness of God produces for the one who allows God to work.

The opening verse is the foundation upon which the rest of the chapter rests. The *therefore* in verse 1 marks the transition from the explanation and defense of justification through faith to the practical aspects of life in Christ as living sacrifices. Verse 1 provides the encouragement, and verse 2 provides the power—a power that comes from the Holy Spirit (note the passive voice of "be transformed"). The consequence is a changed life.

This chapter lists some of the spiritual gifts granted to the children of God, but Paul doesn't spend time explaining them all. His intent is to drive home the point that, in terms of our behavior, only love matters (a major theme for the rest of the letter).

The chapter closes with specific exhortations to love as only those who know Love can. It's interesting to note that many of the things Paul lists here came right out of the mouth of Jesus, especially the Sermon on the Mount (Matthew 5-7).

Before the Meeting

1. Several weeks before this session, arrange for a well-known personality in the community (a sports figure, a local television personality, the mayor, the principal of a local school, or even a highly visible member of your church) to read Romans 12 on video. Make the recording.

MATERIALS NEEDED

- A CD or tape of the song "Rachel Delevoryas" on Randy Stonehill's album *Stories* (Myrrh, 1993)—and a CD player or tape deck
- Overhead transparency of the lyrics to **Rachel Delovoryas** (page 88)—and an overhead projector
- TV, VCR, and a homemade video-tape of a well-known person reading Romans 12 (see **Before the Meeting**, this page, point 1)
- Copies of **A Living Sacrifice** (page 85)
- Copies of **A Private Note to My Rachel Delevoryas** (page 87)
- Blank, unaddressed envelopes (one per student)
- Several No Fear T-shirts (optional; see **For the Younger Set**, page 82)
- 3 x 5 cards (see **Before the Meeting**, this page, point 5)
- This session's **Big Idea** written on a white-board, poster, etc.
- Bibles and pencils (or pens) for all students and adults
- Scripture memory verse cards (page 116)

Gather the students into groups according to school and have them identify one person who is oppressed or shunned. Ask them to formulate a plan to make a difference in his or her life as a group. Encourage them to create a small task force to follow through with their ideas.

▼▼▼▼▼▼▼

2. Get the **Living Sacrifice** worksheet (page 85) and its **Leader's Guide** (page 86) to your small-group leaders a week before the lesson.

3. Write this session's **Big Idea** on a whiteboard, bulletin board, poster, overhead transparency, or wherever it can catch students' eyes during the teaching session. Ideally, after the meeting add this Big Idea to a cumulative list somewhere in the room (perhaps on an empty wall) so your group can track what they've studied in Romans. If you don't have the wall space, use the master on page 115 to make a transparency to project during your review time at the beginning of each session; reveal only the Big Ideas you've studied to date.

4. Cue the tape or CD to "Rachel Delevoryas" and test for volume, clarity, etc. Use the master on page 88 to create a transparency of the lyrics. Check the overhead projector to be sure it works. (Have a spare bulb handy.)

5. Prepare 3 x 5 cards of various roles for Question 5 on the **A Living Sacrifice** worksheet (page 85).

6. Recruit a student to read Romans 12:1-3, 9 at the end of the lesson.

7. Have the groups working from as many different perspectives as possible. If a group seems discouraged by its assignment or gets stuck, let them change. Possible roles can include: sports jock, surfer, rapper, marine, detective, alien, cowboy, and politician. Have the groups read or perform their paraphrases.

Have a No Fear T-shirt design competition. Bring a few No Fear T-shirts and read them to the group. Then divide the group into teams of three to ten people each. Give them five minutes to brainstorm as many No Fear-type slogans as they can that fit the themes presented in Romans 12.

Let them share their slogans, giving prizes in various categories such as the most creative, most number of slogans, and best all-

▼▼▼▼▼▼▼

Opening (20 minutes)

To introduce "Rachel Delevoryas" let the kids know that the song is about a real person although the name and other identifying details have been changed. Project the lyrics with an overhead but keep a piece of paper over the words that haven't been sung so that students follow along with the words.

After playing the song, ask the group to think about and then answer the following questions:

■ **Was Rachel aware that some people felt she was different ("It was clear that she'd never be one of us")? Would she have agreed? Why or why not?**

■ **What words describe how Rachel felt when she heard the boys say, "Rachel is ugly"?**

■ **If you were sitting nearby and saw the whole episode, what might you have done?**

- Assuming similar viciousness goes on all the time, what are some specific, tangible ways we can reach out to the Rachels in our schools and neighborhoods?
- Give the kids an opportunity to mentally identify specific "Rachels" they know. Have a brief period of silent prayer for these people.

Scripture (30 minutes)

Review the Big Ideas from the past eight lessons and display the posters as before. Play the video of the well-known person reading Romans 12. Have students follow along in their Bibles as the video plays.

When the Scripture has been read, hand out copies of **A Living Sacrifice** (page 85). Divide into small groups of six or less, with at least one adult leader per group, to complete the worksheet.

Before the groups get to Question 5, you will need to hand out 3 x 5 cards assigning the group a role to represent as they paraphrase Romans 12:9-21 and present it to the large group.

Application (10 minutes)

Introduce the memory verse and hand out Scripture memory verse cards.

Ask each student to think of a person in his or her school who is different, not well-liked, or is an outcast like Rachel Delevoryas. Read this lesson's Big Idea, followed by a student reading Romans 12:1-3, 9. Give students a few minutes to pray silently about how God would like them to communicate love for the person they thought of.

Hand out the **A Private Note to My Rachel Delevoryas** handout (page 87). Explain the activity in a manner such as:

Write a brief note to the person you just thought of. Tell them something that will express love and care. Encourage them.

Have each student address a blank envelope to himself or herself, put the note inside, seal the envelope, and pass it forward. Plan to mail them to the students a few weeks after this session as reminders of their decisions.

Romans 12:1

Therefore, I urge you, brothers, in view of God's mercy, to offer your bodies as living sacrifices, holy and pleasing to God— this is your spiritual act of worship.

Romans 12:1-21

A Living Sacrifice

1. What's one concrete way to offer your body as a living sacrifice if you are—

A missionary?

A politician?

A business person?

A teacher?

An athlete?

Yourself?

Discuss with your group the ways these ideas can be spiritual acts of worship.

2. Paul writes, "Do not conform any longer to the pattern of this world" (verse 2). What are some specific things that Paul might warn against in your—

Mind

Lifestyle

Speech

Thought life

Dating

Money

Time

3. J. B. Phillips translates verse 2 this way:

Don't let the world squeeze you into its own mold, but let God remold your minds from within.

How do you think these two things can happen?

4. Some spiritual gifts are listed in verses 3-8. Paul's main concern is the attitudes of those who serve God. Even when we use our spiritual gifts, we must act in love.

Write down the names of people you know who may have the gifts listed below, along with one specific example of the gift in action. For example, your mom told you last night how proud she was of your school work—she may be an encourager.

Gift	Who You Know	The Gift in Action
Prophesying (That is, speaking as God's voice in a way that doesn't contradict the Bible)		
Teaching		
Encouraging		
Giving		
Leading		
Showing mercy		

Now let people on your list know what you have observed about them!

5. Your group will receive a 3 x 5 card giving you a role—a personality—to assume while you paraphrase verses 9-21. Work together with your small group. When you're finished, choose a volunteer to present your paraphrase to the class.

Romans 12:1-21
A Living Sacrifice
LEADER'S GUIDE

1 Let each student choose two roles on this list, but make sure every role is included. After they write down their ideas, share them with the group. The question is designed to help students recognize that worship is more than sitting in a pew; it's loving God with all that we are and by everything we do. Service and caring for others is how we live love. Discuss (don't write out) how the suggested actions are spiritual acts of worship.

2 This question will help students to connect real life with the biblical text. Prime their mental pumps by asking questions about the expectations or standards of friends in an area like money or dating. After they have some examples, give them a few minutes to write their own answers, then discuss them together. Once they get the idea, this should be a hot topic.

3 John Stott articulates a three-step process for letting God mold our minds from the inside:

1. Our minds can be renewed by the Holy Spirit and the Bible, which reveal what God's standards are in contrast to the world's standards.
2. We're then able to know God's will.
3. We must be willing to take what we know and allow God to change us through our love for Christ. As Hebrews 3:1 states, "Fix your thoughts on Jesus." Knowledge of God's will is not enough to be transformed. (page 323-4):

This process sets up the rest of Romans 12 and the rest of the book.

4 Most scholars don't believe this chapter contains an exhaustive list of gifts. Romans 12:5, which leads into the passage, reminds us that each member of the body of Christ belongs to all the others and, therefore, we are all obligated to serve, show mercy, encourage, and so forth, even if we don't have those particular spiritual gifts.

5 The leader should assign your group a role. Be loose and creative with this part. Let it be fun!

Romans 12:1-21

A Private Note to My Rachel Delevoryas

This note should not be read by *anyone* except you. It's a reminder to you of how you intend to show love and care toward someone who is different, lonely, or outcast.

_____

_____

_____

_____

_____

_____

_____

_____

_____

_____

_____

_____

_____

_____

_____

_____

Romans 12:1-21
RACHEL DELEVORYAS

Rachel Delevoryas,
  with her thick eyeglasses and her plain Jane face,
Sat beside me in my fifth grade class,
  looking so terribly out of place.
Rachel played the violin, and classical music was out of style.
She couldn't control all her wild brown hair,
  her nervous laughter and her awkward smile.

Chorus:
  It was clear that she'd never be one of us,
  With her dowdy clothes and her violin
  And a name like Rachel Delevoryas.

But I'd pass her house in the evening
  going to play with my best friend, Ray,
And the music floating from her window
  spoke the things that Rachel could never say.
Rachel Delevoryas was eating her lunch as the boys walked by.
"Rachel is ugly!" she heard them shout—
  she sat on the schoolyard bench and cried.

Chorus

And every year the hedge got higher
  as it grew around Rachel's house
Like the secret wall inside her
  that she built to keep all the heartache out
Rachel Delevoryas moved back east with her family
Now she's dressed in a beautiful gown
  standing on stage with the symphony
Rachel plays the violin
  but every night when the lights go down
  I wonder if she still remembers those days
And cruel little boys in this one horse town, and

  It was clear that she'd never be one of us,
  With her dowdy clothes and her violin
  And a name like Rachel Delevoryas.

SESSION TEN

GETTING INVOLVED
Romans 13:1-14

BIG IDEA
Christians are called to be activists, motivated by love.

Overview

Paul's comments in this chapter regarding a believer's response to the governing authorities have been debated since the early church. When Paul writes about submission in verse 1, for example, to what extent does he believe Christians should restrain themselves from challenging civil authority?

Most traditions believe that Christians are called to submit to authority *until* that submission directly violates following Christ. Even the early church met in secret against Roman law, and Paul was certainly aware that some rulers were despots. Yet Paul's greatest concern was the spread of the gospel, and he didn't want anything to hinder believers from sacrificially loving others and spreading the gospel.

Paul's overarching principle for Christians is to care for people—"Clothe yourselves with the Lord Jesus Christ" (verse 14), because that is the fulfillment of the Law.

Before the Meeting

1. Throw your vidcam and a Bible in the car, pick up a few of your students, and head for the first of several sites around town that are fitting backgrounds to a reading of Romans 13. Videotape each of the students reading a section of the chapter. Here are some suggested settings for the readers and the readings:
   - **Verses 1-5:** court building (or inside a court room itself, if you can), police station, or the county jail
   - **Verse 6:** IRS branch, or state or county tax office
   - **Verses 7-10:** a billboard, marquis, etc., on which the word love is prominent
   - **Verses 11-14:** the pornography rack in a convenience store

EXTRA CREDIT

After the meeting have your students take the clothes (from the game Clothes Relay) to a homeless shelter or another facility where the clothes can be put to use. Encourage the students who volunteer to report on what they saw and learned from the experience.

▼▼▼▼▼▼▼

for the YOUNGER SET

Show the clip from *Dead Poets Society* (11:41-16:08 by the counter). In this scene, the English teacher (Robin Williams) challenges his students to "seize the day." Discuss what it means for the kids to seize the day in light of this lesson.

▼▼▼▼▼▼▼

2. Make arrangement to have one student facilitator standing by each sign to lead brainstorming about that topic. The student facilitators will also be responsible for recording the ideas, passing out **Activist pledge cards** cards, and a saying a brief prayer.

3. Preview the video clip if you're using **For the Younger Set** (see box on this page). Cue *Dead Poet's Society* to 11:41. To do this, set the VCR counter on 00:00 as soon as the first credit is shown. Fast forward the video until 11:41 is showing on the machine's counter. Make sure the sound is adjusted and the exact frame on the video is ready to go before the students arrive.

4. Get the **I'm an Activist** worksheet (page 93) and its **Leader's Guide** (page 94) to your small-group leaders a week before the lesson.

5. Write this session's **Big Idea** on a whiteboard, bulletin board, poster, overhead transparency, or wherever it can catch students' eyes during the teaching session. Ideally, after the meeting add this Big Idea to a cumulative list somewhere in the room (perhaps on an empty wall) so your group can track what they've studied in Romans. If you don't have the wall space, use the master on page 115 to make a transparency to project during your review time at the beginning of each session; reveal only the Big Ideas you've studied to date.

6. Copy the **Activist Pledge Cards** master (page 95) onto card-stock and cut the pages in half.

7. Prepare four butcher-paper signs to be taped near the room's four corners later in the session: POLITICS, SCHOOL, COMMUNITY, CHURCH. At that time you'll also tape a blank sheet of butcher paper next to each sign.

8. Gather loose-fitting clothing (shorts, T-shirts, jackets, sweat pants, ties, bathrobes) so that there's at least one item for every student (see **Opening**, this page).

Opening (15 minutes)

To play Clothes Relay, divide the clothes into two piles (each pile with similar kinds of clothes), then divide the class into two teams and line them up at one end of the room ready to race. At the far end of the room, place two similar piles of loose-fitting clothing.

At the signal, the first person from each team runs to the clothes, chooses anything, puts it on, runs back to the second runner, and takes off the piece of clothing from the pile.

The next person in line must put on the clothing brought back by the first one before returning to the stock pile to put on another item. The second runner returns to meet the third student, and the relay continues with an ever-increasing wardrobe.

The first team to have all the players participate as described is declared the winner. Reward them with small prizes.

Scripture (25 minutes)

Review the **Big Ideas** from Sessions 1-9 and display them as before. Have students follow along in their Bibles while you play the video of students from the class reading Romans 13 in front of various places of social concern, (an abortion clinic, the police station, a homeless shelter). Following the video, hand out **Be an Activist!** worksheets (page 95) and pens. Break into small groups of six or fewer students, with at least one adult leader in each to complete the worksheet.

Application (20 minutes)

While students are working in small groups, tape up the signs and butcher paper near the corners of the room. Leave a marker nearby.

When the groups are finished with their worksheets, bring everyone together. Introduce the four areas, then let the kids go to the one that interests them the most as a realm where they can tangibly express their faith. The student facilitators at each station can moderate a brief brainstorming session on the topic by asking the question, "How can we make an impact in this area?" Ideas should not be evaluated at this time; encourage the kids to shout out whatever ideas come to mind. Often one crazy idea sparks a thought that leads to an idea that works perfectly. Someone in each group should record all ideas on the butcher paper.

After a few minutes of gathering ideas at the stations, have the student leaders hand out **Activist Pledge Cards** (page 95) to everyone in their group. Each student should choose an idea from the brainstorming session that he or she would be willing to do.

Bring the group back together for a brief period of sharing students' choices.

Introduce the memory verse, hand out verse cards, review the Big Idea, and refer to the poster.

Close by having each of the four student leaders say a brief prayer for the area he or she facilitated, followed by silence for private prayer.

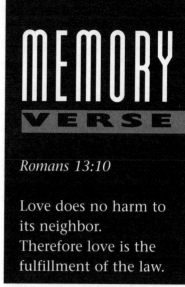

MEMORY VERSE

Romans 13:10

Love does no harm to its neighbor. Therefore love is the fulfillment of the law.

Be an Activist!

I. In verses 1-6, what's the key phrase (Paul's main point)?

What are three reasons he gives for doing this?

1.

2.

3.

2. Look at Jesus' words to the Roman governor, Pontius Pilate, recorded in John 19:11. Does this mean that God personally appointed him to rule?   ❏ Yes   ❏ No

How about Hitler, Stalin, and Saddam?   ❏ Yes   ❏ No

Why or why not?

3. Compare Romans 13:1-5 and Acts 5:25-29. Now check AGREE or DISAGREE about the following statement:

We're to submit to civil authorities unless we would be disobeying God by doing so.

❏ AGREE   ❏ DISAGREE

Why?

If you agree, what's an example of a time when this may be true?

4. Verses 6 and 7 are applications of Paul's teaching in this chapter. List the four areas mentioned and give examples of where or how they apply to Christians today.

AREA   **EXAMPLE**

1.

2.

3.

4.

5. As followers of Jesus Christ, we're called to be activists with our faith. What important things are we to keep in mind?

1.

2.

Romans 13:1-14
Be an Activist!
LEADER'S GUIDE

According to John Stott, in this chapter of Romans

> Paul enlarges on the state's God-appointed role and on the role of Christian people in relation to it, although his emphasis is on personal citizenship rather than on any particular theory of church-state relations (page 339).

This lesson centers on the individual believer's responsibility to be active with love. Students can complete the worksheet individually before discussing it.

1 Paul's main point in verses 1-6 is that Christians, as a general rule, should submit to the governing authorities. He gives three reasons:

■ God established them
■ So we can be free from fear
■ The authority is God's servant, so we will be submitting to God

2 Few would say that God appointed such obvious criminals. According to John Stott,

> Paul means rather that all human authority is derived from God's authority (page 340).

Paul knew that unjust rulers were rampant, but he was directing Christ's followers to do their best to live in peace with all governing authorities.

3 Allow students to discuss the statement. To agree is consistent with Paul's overall theology. The crux of the argument: at what point has civil authority gone too far? For some, it's legalizing abortion; for others, military service. Encourage the students to discuss what they think, rather than telling them what to believe.

4 The four things mentioned in verses 6 and 7 are taxes, money (revenue), respect, and honor. Modern examples include paying taxes, taking out loans, respecting police, and honoring veterans.

5 The two things to emphasize from this chapter:

■ We must obey all authority until obedience would violate our loyalty to God.
■ Love must be both our motivation and our action.

Romans 13:1-14

Activist Pledge Cards

Because God has called me to be an *activist, with love,* my goal is to make a difference in

_____
(area of interest or skill)

by doing the following actions:

1. _____

_____

2. _____

_____

Signature _____ Date _____

Because God has called me to be an *activist, with love,* my goal is to make a difference in

_____
(area of interest or skill)

by doing the following actions:

1. _____

_____

2. _____

_____

Signature _____ Date _____

SESSION ELEVEN

WE'RE ONE!
Romans 14:1-23

BIG IDEA
God calls the body of Christ to be unified.

MATERIALS NEEDED

- 5 student actors, and 5 copies of the sketch **My Youth Group** (pages 103-104)
- Props for the sketch (see prop list, page 103)
- Vidcam and blank videotape, to record the performance of the sketch (optional; see **Extra Credit**, page 98)
- Copies of **My Youth Group, Revisited** (page 105)
- Homemade audio recording of children reading Romans 14, and a tape deck (see **Before the Meeting**, page 98, point 3)
- Copies of **We're One in Christ** (page 101)
- This session's **Big Idea** written on a whiteboard, poster, etc.
- Bibles and pencils (or pens) for all students and adults
- Scripture memory verse cards (page 116)

Overview

Chapter 14 contains Paul's well-known admonition to strong believers, instructing them not to cause Jewish Christians to struggle with the freedom the Gentile believers were exercising in Christ. (This chapter is similar to 1 Corinthians 8, which deals with the specific issue of whether to eat meat offered to idols, and its effect on some Christians.)

Paul's argument focuses on a certain kind of weakness. According to Stott, he doesn't mean a weakness of either

> will or of character, but of faith (14:1). So if we're trying to picture a weaker brother or sister, we must not envision a vulnerable Christian easily overcome by temptation, but a sensitive Christian full of indecision and scruples (page 355).

The problem is not self-control, but conscience. Though there are differing theories concerning Paul's meaning, perhaps the best explanation is that he's referring to Jewish Christians who had chosen to follow Jesus as Messiah, but who were having a hard time giving up the rigors of Jewish religious tradition.

Paul's main point is found in verses 19 and 22, where he exhorts the family of believers to do whatever leads to peace and to keep personal preferences private.

His final statement is a warning to the strong—"Everything that does not come from faith is sin" (verse 23).

In other words, you should be certain that your behavior and choices do not compel another Christian—especially a newer or weaker Christian—into similar behavior, whose rightness that Christian may doubt. (This passage has nothing to do with others merely agreeing or disagreeing with the rightness of your behavior.)

Before the Meeting

1. Several weeks before the lesson, recruit five students to present the sketch **My Youth Group** (pages 103-104). Get the scripts to them right away so they can rehearse at least twice before the performance. The play isn't long, but to be effective, the performers must know their lines.

    Have the students in the drama set up the stage before the session begins so they can start right after the opening game and discussion.

2. Get the **We're One in Christ** worksheet (page 101) and its **Leader's Guide** (page 102) to your small-group leaders a week before the lesson.

3. Write this session's **Big Idea** on a whiteboard, bulletin board, poster, overhead transparency, or wherever it can catch students' eyes during the teaching session. Ideally, after the meeting add this Big Idea to a cumulative list somewhere in the room (perhaps on an empty wall) so your group can track what they've studied in Romans. If you don't have the wall space, use the master on page 115 to make a transparency to project during your review time at the beginning of each session; reveal only the Big Ideas you've studied to date.

4. Arrange for several small children who can read fairly well to be recorded reading Romans 14 on an audiocassette.

Opening (10 minutes)

Play the game Would You Rather...? Have students break into groups of two or three. Read the first question from the list below and give the small groups one minute to discuss it.

Call out "Switch!" Everyone finds a new group of two or three for the next question. Repeat the procedure with a new question.

- ■ **Would you rather be in jail for a month or on a deserted island for a year?**
- ■ **Would you rather be famous or rich?**
- ■ **Would you rather have one steady boyfriend or girlfriend and no other friends, or many friends but no steady?**
- ■ **Would you rather be deaf or blind?***

As a follow-up to this activity, ask for the most unusual responses.

*There are hundreds more of these discussion starters in *Would You Rather...? 465 Provocative Questions to Get Teenagers Talking* (Youth Specialties). Order by calling 800/776-8008.

Activity: Drama (10 minutes)

Have the actors perform the sketch **My Youth Group** (pages 103-104).
After the drama, ask the following questions:

- ■ **Who was the best person? Why?**
- ■ **Who was the worst person? Why?**
- ■ **What made Jill so upset? Did she have a good reason?**
- ■ **Do you think this kind of thing ever happens at your school (or in your town or neighborhood)?**

Scripture (30 minutes)

Review the **Big Ideas** from the past ten lessons and display them up front as before. Have the students turn to Romans 14 in their Bibles to follow along as you play the audiotape of the children reading the passage.

Break into small groups of six or fewer students with at least one adult leader per group. Hand out the **We're One in Christ** worksheets (page 101) and have the kids complete them.

Application (10 minutes)

When the students have finished, bring them back together. Introduce the memory verse, hand out the verse cards, review the Big Idea and refer to the poster.

Hand out **My Youth Group, Revisited** worksheets (page 105) for students to fill out.

Close with a time of tag-team prayer—one person begins a prayer, another person picks up where he or she left off, and so on.

MEMORY VERSE

Romans 14:13

Therefore let us stop passing judgment on one another. Instead, make up your mind not to put any stumbling block or obstacle in your brother's way.

▼ ▼ ▼ ▼ ▼ ▼ ▼

Romans 14:1-23
We're One in Christ

---

1. In this chapter, Paul defines the weak as — (check the best answer)

❑ a. physically weak or sick
❑ b. a sensitive Christian who lacks freedom of conscience
❑ c. someone who is wrong
❑ d. a vulnerable Christian easily overcome by temptation

2. Paul calls diet (food and drink) and the day of worship disputable matters (verses 1, 5). Check the things on the list below that you think modern Christians may have differing opinions about.

❑ Smoking   ❑ Eating red meat and fat
❑ Alcohol   ❑ Speeding
❑ Swearing   ❑ Racist jokes
❑ Illegal drugs   ❑ Pollution
❑ Home schooling   ❑ Style of worship
❑ Critical gossip about other Christian groups
❑ Material possessions (size of house, kind of car, etc.)

3. List the top five areas (from the list above list) that we should avoid passing judgment on one another.

1.

2.

3.

4.

5.

Why did you pick these?

4. Verse 13 refers to the strong believer's attitude (don't pass judgement) as well as actions (don't put stumbling blocks in a brother's way). What reasons does he give?

1. (verse 14-16)

2. (verse 17-21)

5. What's Paul's final advice regarding these disputable matters?

Romans 14:1-23
We're One in Christ
LEADER'S GUIDE

1 According to John Stott, **b.** is the most likely answer. The weak were probably Jewish Christians, or Gentiles who were strongly influenced by Jewish practices, who kept the Old Testament food laws—eating only clean items—as well as the sacred nature of the Sabbath.

2 and 3 These two questions can generate discussion on the differences between what are matters of conscience, and what are matters clearly defined as contrary to the gospel. Here's an example of how the list might be distributed (this is only an example—you know what your church, your kids, and your conscious can tolerate):

■ **Against the law, therefore not disputable:** (see Romans 13) use of or dealing in illegal drugs, underage drinking of alcohol, curfew

■ **Harmful, arrogant, or lacking in love—so also not disputable:** profanity, off-color and racist jokes, disobedience to parent, any form of academic cheating, premarital sexual activity

■ **Not clearly defined, therefore disputable:** use of tobacco and alcohol (provided users are not minors), pollution, kind and quantity of material possessions, eating red meat and fats, home schooling

    A person's convictions about items in this third category, Paul writes, are difficult to condemn.

4 The two foundational reasons for strong believers guarding their attitudes and their actions:

■ (verse 14-16) If they don't, they're violating the law of love (see Matthew 22:37-40).

■ (verse 17-21) It can hinder God's work in the person, and therefore in the world.

5 Paul's final advice with these disputable matters is to act in secret. God often works through the believer's conscience (although this is obviously not an infallible determiner of right and wrong). In disputable matters we all must continually challenge our thinking.

Romans 14:1-23

my youth group

Cast

Five students the same age as the audience. Male and female roles may be switched if necessary.

Jill, *interested in Christianity, wants to find out more, hurting*

Mike, *an officer of Cool Life, a fun campus club that several popular students attend*

Karla, *a home-schooler, attends a small church with no youth group*

Noel, *active in Workout Community Church's outreach ministry*

Rene, *carries her Bible everywhere, active at First Conservative Church*

Setting

All these students live in the same neighborhood. They have known each other for a while. The scene opens in an ice cream shop where Noel is wiping down a table, Rene and Karla are sitting together looking at a Bible, and Jill is studying at as separate table. Mike is offstage.

Props

Three tables • Ice cream • Three chairs • A cleaning cloth
Bowls • A Bible • Spoons • An apron for Noel • Books for Jill

---

Rene: Listen to this: "Accept him whose faith is weak." I knew it was in here! See, I told you that God says you can be weak and still be a Christian . . . but obviously not a very committed one!

Karla: I'm not sure that's true, Rene. I mean, I read the Bible four hours a day, and it just seems to me that if you don't really give your whole life to the Lord and read the Word and pray without ceasing, you really aren't much of a Christian. *(Jill overhears this conversation; she continues to read, but occasionally glances over at the others, interested)*

Rene: You know what I mean, though. Oh, sure, we're supposed to read our Bibles and stuff like that, but it's a lot more important to not be weak, and to not have false doctrine. My church, First Conservative Church, gives us a list of all the things that make you strong so you don't end up weak *(looks toward Noel, smiling sarcastic)* like Noel over there.

Karla: No, Rene! To be strong means to devote yourself to God every minute, like I do. What you know is important, but it's much more important how devoted you are to God, like me! *(looking at Noel)* Doesn't he go to that weird church, Workout Community? I heard they only have services on Sundays, and they don't even encourage daily Quiet Times!

Noel: *(walking over)* Hey, I heard that, Karla. You guys just don't get it, do you? We've got a great church. We know how to worship, that's for sure. You guys've got it all wrong. You, Rene—at First Conservative over there—I used to go to that church. I learned a lot—hey, I'm not down on it—but when are you guys gonna learn how to worship?

Rene: We worship in the Word, not with a tennis racquet!

Noel: Hey, the Bible's our book, too, but we'd rather live it then eat it! We've got so many people comin' to Jesus, God's head's spinnin'! Why, our youth group...

Karla: That's the problem, Noel. You guys spend so much time singing and playing games at your youth group that you don't have any time left to devote yourselves to the Lord. I memorize ten verses a week, and my pastor preaches as God leads, and that means he doesn't even get warmed up until noon! Both of you only worship for an hour! How can God speak to you?

Rene: God is a God of order and purpose—that's in his Word. I don't want to get weak by loose singing, and we...

Mike: *(enters)* Hi, you guys! Are you coming to the pizza bash? Everybody will be there! Tommy, Sue, Jack...

Karla: It sounds like a party.

Mike: It is! It is a party! We're gonna party all night! We'll show everybody that Christians can have fun and still love God.

Noel: You know, Mike, the problem with those parties at Cool Life is you aren't connected to a church. There can't be any real evangelism when you're not connected to the church. Real evangelism is a strategy—attract people to the church, touch their felt needs, and—WHAM—hit 'em with the gospel! Boom! They're hooked, just like a fish!

Mike: Hey, we tell 'em about Jesus, but we don't need a strategy, just a relationship! We just take our time, ease 'em into it. You guys can't understand that because you don't know any non-Christians. People are sick of Christians, so we show 'em that God likes to party, too! *(all four are getting more and more agitated; Jill is watching, occasionally shaking her head, but nobody notices her)*

Rene: I'm not sure that you guys aren't doing more harm than good—the Bible is what needs to be taught and studied. What doctrines do you teach at Cool Life?

Karla: *(aside)* He can't even spell <u>doctrines.</u>

Mike: We don't need any doctrines, Rene—all we need is Jesus—and relationships. That's all that matters.

Noel: But it can't work outside the church.

Mike: It sure can, and it does, a lot better than you.

Rene: You're both wrong. God is a God of order, and what he wants is his Word preached with proper doctrine.

Karla: All of you are weak. Look how you argue. You need more time in prayer and solitude, less youth groups and parties and doctrine. *(almost at once, rapidly interrupting each other)*

Rene: Hey, wait a minute—

Noel: You don't know anything.

Mike: You're so out of touch. *(They all start arguing; Jill slams her book on the table and starts to cry; everyone stops and stares, first at her, then at each other; finally Noel goes over and tries to sit down, but she stops him)*

Jill: *(trying to keep from crying)* Don't try your WHAM-just-like-a-fish stuff on me, Noel. Get away from me! You all make me sick. *(standing up, confronting the four)* I just found out my parents are getting a divorce, and I figured that one of you could help me understand it. That's why I came over here today. I know you guys are the so-called Christians, and you usually hang out here, so I wanted to know how God can help me through this. But after hearing you fight and argue and complain, I don't want anything to do with any of you. *(she runs out crying)*

Rene: *(after a shaky silence)* I should have read her a verse.

Karla: She needs to repent.

Mike: She ought to come to the party tonight.

Noel: She needs a seminar on healthy self-image. *(they look at each other, and all at once say loudly)*

ALL: You're all wrong!! *(they all storm out in different directions)*

— *END* —

Romans 14:1-23

my youth group
REVISITED

We're called to unity in the body of Christ (the Big Idea for Romans 14). Yet what's the biggest obstacle—if there is one—that each person must overcome to fulfill the Big Idea?

- Mike — An officer of Cool Life (a campus club that is fun, has games, and has several popular students attending)
- Karla — A home-schooled student who attends a small church with no youth group
- Noel — Very active in Workout Community Church's outreach youth ministry
- Rene — Carries her Bible everywhere, very active in the youth group at First Conservative Church

As you consider yourself and this lesson, finish these two sentences:

- With regard to the unity I'm called to in Christ, the biggest problem I have right now is—

- One thing I'm going to do about my problem is—

SESSION TWELVE

UNIFIED IN LOVE
Romans 15:1-16:27

BIG IDEA
Love is what keeps the body of Christ unified.

Overview

Paul begins the final two chapters by summarizing his call to unity in the body of Christ, especially between Jewish and Gentile Christians (15:1-13). He then reaffirms his calling to the Gentiles (15:14-22) and closes the fifteenth chapter by laying out his plans to visit them.

Chapter 16 is personal; verses 1-16 are specific greetings to various people with whom Paul had worked. The list is varied, and—as ancient literature—is astounding in singling out women.

Chapter 16, verses 17-20, is a final call to unity and a warning to avoid divisions in the family of God. Paul then hands the letter over to those with whom he's traveling, allowing Tertius to mention that he was the scribe who recorded the words of Paul. The letter concludes with Paul praising the eternal God.

Before the Meeting

1. Call for brochures from Compassion International and World Vision if you're planning to discuss supporting a child through one of those organizations.
2. Preview the video clip from *Roxanne* to determine its suitability for your group. By the VCR counter, the segment starts at 25:15. That's the scene in which Roxanne and C.D. (a modern Cyrano de Bergerac) walk up a mountain, and C.D. discovers that she doesn't love him; C.D. goes immediately to a plastic surgeon about getting his nose shortened. To cue the video by the VCR counter, set the counter on 00:00 when the first credit appears. Then fast-forward to 25:15. Cue up the video and adjust the sound before students arrive. (If you have time for pure hilarity unrelated to the session, show the fireman-training segment that immediately precedes this episode.)

MATERIALS
NEEDED

- TV, VCR, and the video *Roxanne* (1987, PG)
- 3 x 5 cards (see **Before the Meeting**, this page, point 3)
- Copies of **One Lord, One Body** (page 111)
- Brochures from Compassion International, World Vision, etc. (optional; see **Extra Credit**, page 108)
- Copies of **A Letter to Jesus** (page 113)
- Blank, unaddressed envelopes (one per student)
- This session's **Big Idea** written on a whiteboard, poster, etc.
- Bibles and pencils (or pens) for all students and adults
- Scripture memory verse cards (page 116)

3. Recruit as many students as you would like—the more, the better—to be Scripture readers. Divide the passage into small sections of several verses each. On paper assign students numbers so everyone knows their positions for reading. Prepare 3 x 5 cards for each student with the following information:

   ■ the student's number
   ■ the name and number of the person he or she will read after (so students will know when it's their turns)
   ■ the passages they are to read (you don't need to type them out, just list the verses they will be reading)
   ■ phonetic spellings of any words or names in that they may find difficult (such as the names in chapter 16).

   Have students practice their passages before the meeting.

4. Get the **One Lord, One Body** worksheet (page 111) and its **Leader's Guide** (page 112) to your small-group leaders a week before the lesson.

5. Write this session's Big Idea on a whiteboard, bulletin board, poster, overhead transparency, or wherever it can catch students' eyes during the teaching session. Ideally, after the meeting add this Big Idea to a cumulative list somewhere in the room (perhaps on an empty wall) so your group can track what they've studied in Romans. If you don't have the wall space, use the master on page 115 to make a transparency to project during your review time at the beginning of each session; reveal only the Big Ideas you've studied to date.

Opening (15 minutes)

Show the clip from *Roxanne*—beginning at 25:15 on the counter. Introduce the clip with comments such as the following:

C.D., played by Steve Martin, is one of the most friendly, popular guys in town. He's fallen in love with Roxanne, played by Daryl Hannah. In the scene we're going to watch, she's asked C.D. to take a hike with her. He thinks she's going to tell him she loves him.

After watching the video, ask the teens the following questions:

■ **Was C.D.'s nose really the reason Roxanne wasn't in love with him?**
■ **Is it fair that a man or woman wouldn't be loved because he or she has an unusual physical trait, even with a great personality?**
■ **Is it common?**
■ **What would it would feel like to be C.D. with a nose like that?**

Connect this clip to the lesson by saying something like—

> **Even among Christians, there are often attitudes like what we have just seen—judging people by how they look. One of the main reasons Paul wrote the letter to the Roman believers was to call them to a new standard of living—to love and unity.**
>
> **Even in churches there are people who feel different, unloved, and separated from others. As followers of Jesus, who are all members of the same family, we should do all we can to break down those walls that hurt and separate, by honoring and respecting people who are different—just like we want to be treated.**

Scripture (30 minutes)

Review the past eleven **Big Ideas** and display them as in all the past lessons.

Have the class open their Bibles to the passage and follow along while the volunteers read their passages, using the 3 x 5 cards. This passage should be read popcorn style—the first student stands to read his or her few verses and then sits down. The second reader pops up right away to participate, and so on until the chapters have been read.

Break up into small groups of six or less with at least one adult leader per group. Hand out **One Lord, One Body** worksheets (page 111) and pens for the students to complete.

When the kids have completed the worksheets, gather the class back together. Have the groups share comments made during their discussions of Question 7.

Application (15 minutes)

Introduce the memory verse, hand out the verse cards, restate the Big Idea, and refer to the poster.

Hand out **A Letter to Jesus** (page 113) and blank envelopes. Instruct the kids to use their letters to let Jesus know what they have learned from this lesson, or the entire series. Invite them to share their ideas if they're willing to. After sharing, they should seal the letters in the envelopes and put their names on the outside.

Close the session by having students return to their small groups to pray for one another. As they leave, collect the letters. Mail them to the students within a few weeks, accompanied by a cover letter from you, summarizing what you hope they remember from Romans, along with a poster-sized list of the 12 Big Ideas. You can enlarge the master on page 114 and copy it onto bright paper.

Romans 15:1-16:27
One LORD, One BODY

1. Paul prays that God's gift of endurance and encouragement would give the Roman believers a spirit of unity (15:5). What does "a spirit of unity" looks like to you?

How could endurance and encouragement from God give you this kind of unity with other Christians?

2. In what three areas does Paul express confidence in the Roman believers (15:14)?

1.

2.

3.

3. Paul closes the letter the way he opened it—with great personal confidence (15:15-22). Write brief descriptions of three times when you pleased God.

1.

2.

3.

4. The early churches gave lots of money to the poor, especially poor Christians (15:26-28). Why do they owe their money and material possessions to these poorer believers?

How could a giving ethic affect your life?

5. In the closing (Chapter 16), Paul mentions many people. How many are mentioned?

How many men?

How many women?

How many are there that could be either?

What can you learn about Paul from this list?

6. Who actually wrote down the letter to the Romans (16:22)?

Why do we say that Paul wrote it?

7. What's the last thing Paul teaches about in 16:17-19?

Why does Paul conclude this way?

Romans 15:1-16:27
One LORD, One BODY
LEADER'S GUIDE

Ask the students to complete the worksheet on their own. When they're finished, discuss it as a group.

1 Helpful guidance for this question is in 15:7: "Accept one another, then, just as Christ accepted you, in order to bring praise to God." As we grow in our faith (endurance) and are reminded of God's unconditional love (encouragement), it's far easier to be gentle, forgiving, and accepting of others.

2 and 3 If your students find these questions difficult to understand or answer, guide a discussion about what it means to have a healthy view of one's self, based on being God's creation and his work in believers through the Spirit. More students will be critical of themselves than overly inflated. Paul seemed to find the balance, based on Christ, and not on his own merits.

4 This passage is a window into the New Testament view of tithing—10 percent may be a good general guideline, but as believers, our giving is based on others' needs and the resources God has given us. Since the body of Christ is a family, bound together in unity, we're now called to care for each other, which includes sharing our material wealth (see Matthew 6 for Jesus' comments on this). This may be a good time to bring up supporting a child through Compassion International or World Vision (refer to **Extra Credit** on page 108).

5 Of the 27 people Paul mentions in chapter 16, at least 10 are women: In addition to Phoebe, there's Priscilla (verse 3), Mary (verse 6), probably Junias (verse 7), Tryphena (verse 12), Tryphosa (verse 12), Persis (verse 12), Rufus' mother (verse 13), Julia (verse 15), and Nereus' sister (verse 15). Paul apparently thinks highly of them all. He singled out four women—and no men—who worked hard: Mary, Tryphena, Tryphosa, and Persis.

6 Tertius, a man we know nothing about, actually wrote the letter; Paul dictated it to him.

7 The last substantial teaching in Romans (16:17-19) concerns unity—ultimately the theme of the entire book.

Romans 15:1-16:27

A Letter to Jesus

_____
(date)

Dear Jesus,

I've been reading Romans lately, and I want you to know that I've learned—

Because of the things we've studied and talked about, the way I'm going to put this knowledge into practice is—

If there's one thing I need from you right now, it's—

Love,

_____
(your name)

SUMMARY OF BIG IDEAS IN ROMANS

SESSION ▼	PASSAGE ▼	
One	1:1-17	God is at work in our lives to make us pleasing and useful to him.
Two	1:18–3:31	Every person is a rebel, but God has made a way to change us through faith.
Three	4:1-25	Faith is having confidence that God is still working on me.
Four	5:1-21	Real faith brings peace with God.
Five	6:1-23	Because you die only once, live for Christ now.
Six	7:1-25	Sin is a battle, but the war has been won.
Seven	8:1-39	In Christ we're more than conquerors.
Eight	9:1–11:36	We do not support the root—the root supports us.
Nine	12:1-21	We express our love for God by sacrificially loving others.
Ten	13:1-14	Christians are called to be activists, motivated by love.
Eleven	14:1-23	God calls the body of Christ to be unified.
Twelve	15:1–16:27	Love is what keeps the body of Christ unified.

THE BIG IDEAS IN ROMANS

God is at work in our lives to make us pleasing and useful to him. (1:1-17)

Every person is a rebel, but God has made a way to change us through faith. (1:18–3:31)

Faith is having confidence that God is still working on me. (4:1-25)

Real faith brings peace with God. (5:1-21)

Because you die only once, live for Christ now. (6:1-23)

Sin is a battle, but the war has been won. (7:1-25)

In Christ we're more than conquerors. (8:1-39)

We do not support the root—the root supports us. (9:1–11:36)

We express our love for God by sacrificially loving others. (12:1-21)

Christians are called to be activists, motivated by love. (13:1-14)

God calls the body of Christ to be unified. (14:1-23)

Love is what keeps the body of Christ unified. (15:1–16:27)

SCRIPTURE
MEMORY VERSE
CARDS

Romans 1:17
For in the gospel a righteousness from God is revealed, a righteousness that is by faith from first to last, just as it is written: "The righteous will live by faith."

Romans 3:22
This righteousness from God comes through Jesus Christ to all who believe.

Romans 4:5
To the man who does not work but trusts God who justifies the wicked, his faith is credited as righteousness.

Romans 5:3-5
We also rejoice in our sufferings, because we know that suffering produces perseverance; perseverance, character; and character, hope. And hope does not disappoint us, because God has poured out his love into our hearts by the Holy Spirit, whom he has given us.

Romans 6:11
Count yourselves dead to sin but alive to God in Jesus Christ.

Romans 7:4
So, my brothers, you also died to the law through the body of Christ, that you might belong to another, to him who was raised from the dead, in order that we might bear fruit to God.

Romans 8:31
What, then, shall we say in response to this? If God is for us, who can be against us?

Romans 11:33
Oh, the depth of the riches of the wisdom and knowledge of God! How unsearchable his judgements, and his paths beyond tracing out!

Romans 12:1
Therefore, I urge you, brothers, in view of God's mercy, to offer your bodies as living sacrifices, holy and pleasing to God—this is your spiritual act of worship.

Romans 13:10
Love does no harm to its neighbor. Therefore love is the fulfillment of the law.

Romans 14:13
Therefore let us stop passing judgement on one another. Instead, make up your mind not to put up any stumbling block or obstacle in your brother's way.

Romans 15:4
For everything that was written in the past was written to teach us, so that through the endurance and the encouragement of the Scriptures we might have hope.

Resources from Youth Specialties

Professional Resources

Administration, Publicity, & Fundraising (Ideas Library)
Developing Student Leaders
Equipped to Serve: Volunteer Youth Worker Training Course
Help! I'm a Junior High Youth Worker!
Help! I'm a Small-Group Leader!
Help! I'm a Sunday School Teacher!
Help! I'm a Volunteer Youth Worker!
How to Expand Your Youth Ministry
How to Speak to Youth...and Keep Them Awake at the Same Time
Junior High Ministry (Updated & Expanded)
The Ministry of Nurture: A Youth Worker's Guide to Discipling Teenagers
One Kid at a Time: Reaching Youth through Mentoring
Purpose-Driven Youth Ministry
So *That's* Why I Keep Doing This! 52 Devotional Stories for Youth Workers
A Youth Ministry Crash Course
The Youth Worker's Handbook to Family Ministry

Youth Ministry Programming

Camps, Retreats, Missions, & Service Ideas (Ideas Library)
Compassionate Kids: Practical Ways to Involve Your Students in Mission and Service
Creative Bible Lessons from the Old Testament
Creative Bible Lessons in 1 & 2 Corinthians
Creative Bible Lessons in John: Encounters with Jesus
Creative Bible Lessons in Romans: Faith on Fire!
Creative Bible Lessons on the Life of Christ
Creative Junior High Programs from A to Z, Vol. 1 (A-M)
Creative Junior High Programs from A to Z, Vol. 2 (N-Z)
Creative Meetings, Bible Lessons, & Worship Ideas (Ideas Library)
Crowd Breakers & Mixers (Ideas Library)
Drama, Skits, & Sketches (Ideas Library)
Drama, Skits, & Sketches 2 (Ideas Library)
Dramatic Pauses
Everyday Object Lessons
Games (Ideas Library)
Games 2 (Ideas Library)
Great Fundraising Ideas for Youth Groups
More Great Fundraising Ideas for Youth Groups
Great Retreats for Youth Groups
Greatest Skits on Earth
Greatest Skits on Earth, Vol. 2
Holiday Ideas (Ideas Library)
Hot Illustrations for Youth Talks
More Hot Illustrations for Youth Talks
Still More Hot Illustrations for Youth Talks
Incredible Questionnaires for Youth Ministry
Junior High Game Nights
More Junior High Game Nights

Kickstarters: 101 Ingenious Intros to Just about Any Bible Lesson
Live the Life! Student Evangelism Training Kit
Memory Makers
Play It! Great Games for Groups
Play It Again! More Great Games for Groups
Special Events (Ideas Library)
Spontaneous Melodramas
Super Sketches for Youth Ministry
Teaching the Bible Creatively
The Next Level: Youth Leader's Kit
Videos That Teach
Wild Truth Bible Lessons
Wild Truth Bible Lessons 2
Wild Truth Bible Lessons—Pictures of God
Worship Services for Youth Groups

Discussion Starters

Discussion & Lesson Starters (Ideas Library)
Discussion & Lesson Starters 2 (Ideas Library)
Get 'Em Talking
Keep 'Em Talking!
High School TalkSheets
More High School TalkSheets
High School TalkSheets: Psalms and Proverbs
Junior High TalkSheets
More Junior High TalkSheets
Junior High TalkSheets: Psalms and Proverbs
What If...? 450 Thought-Provoking Questions to Get Teenagers Talking, Laughing, and Thinking
Would You Rather...? 465 Provocative Questions to Get Teenagers Talking
Have You Ever...? 450 Intriguing Questions Guaranteed to Get Teenagers Talking

Clip Art

ArtSource: Stark Raving Clip Art (print)
ArtSource: Youth Group Activities (print)
ArtSource CD-ROM: Clip Art Library Version 2.0

Videos

EdgeTV
The Heart of Youth Ministry: A Morning with Mike Yaconelli
Next Time I Fall in Love Video Curriculum
Purpose Driven Youth Ministry Video Curriculum
Understanding Your Teenager Video Curriculum

Student Books

Grow For It Journal
Grow For It Journal through the Scriptures
Spiritual Challenge Journal: The Next Level
Teen Devotional Bible
What Would Jesus Do? Spiritual Challenge Journal
Wild Truth Journal for Junior Highers
Wild Truth Journal—Pictures of God